FASHION SKETCHBOOK

Male Figure Template

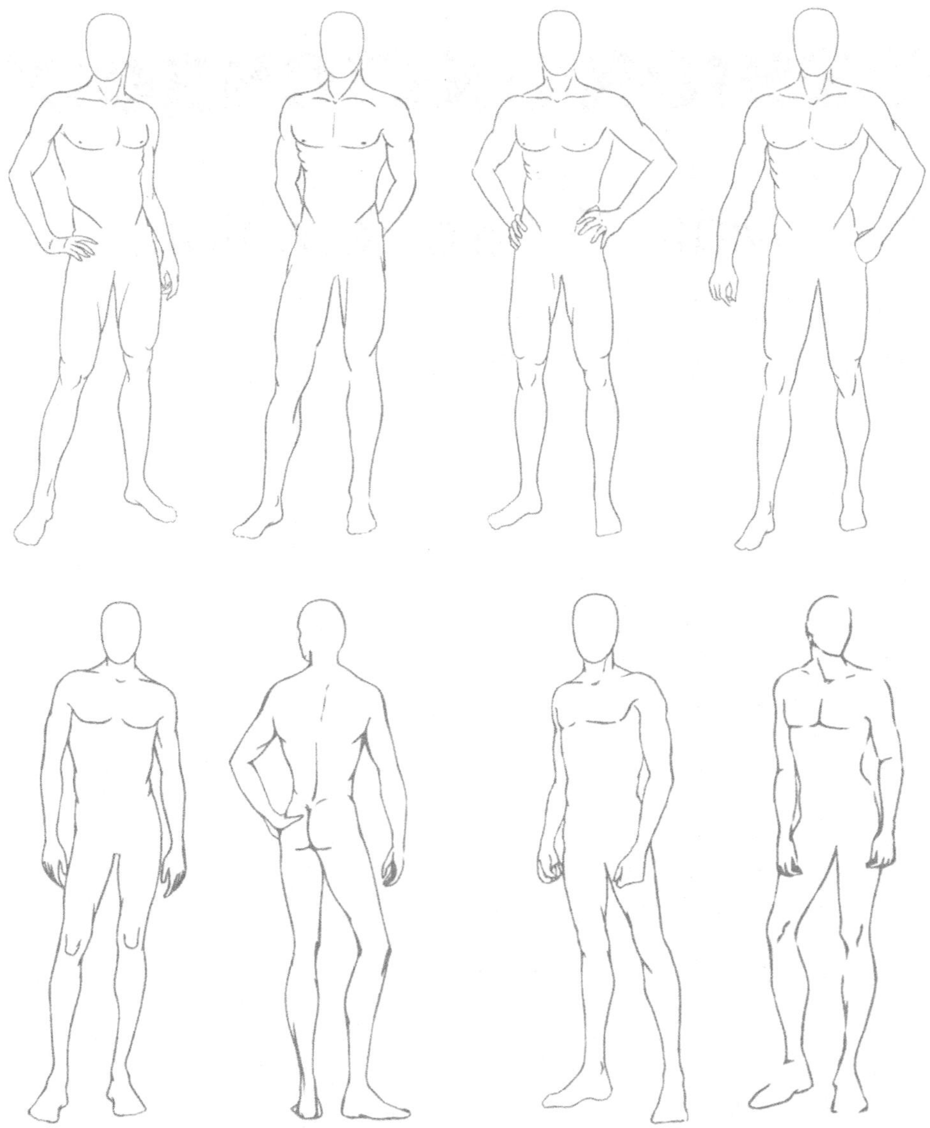

Lance Publishing Studio
Lance Derrick
lancepublish.com

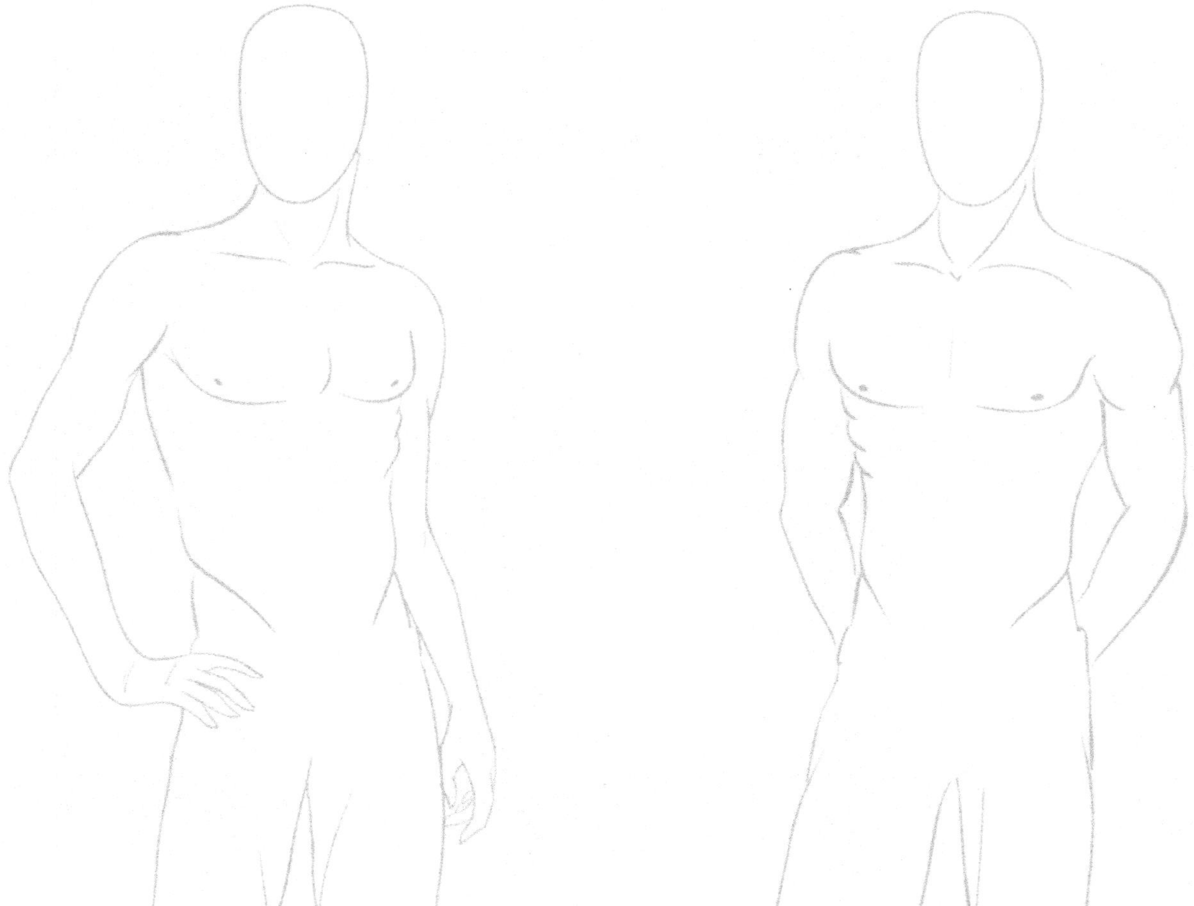

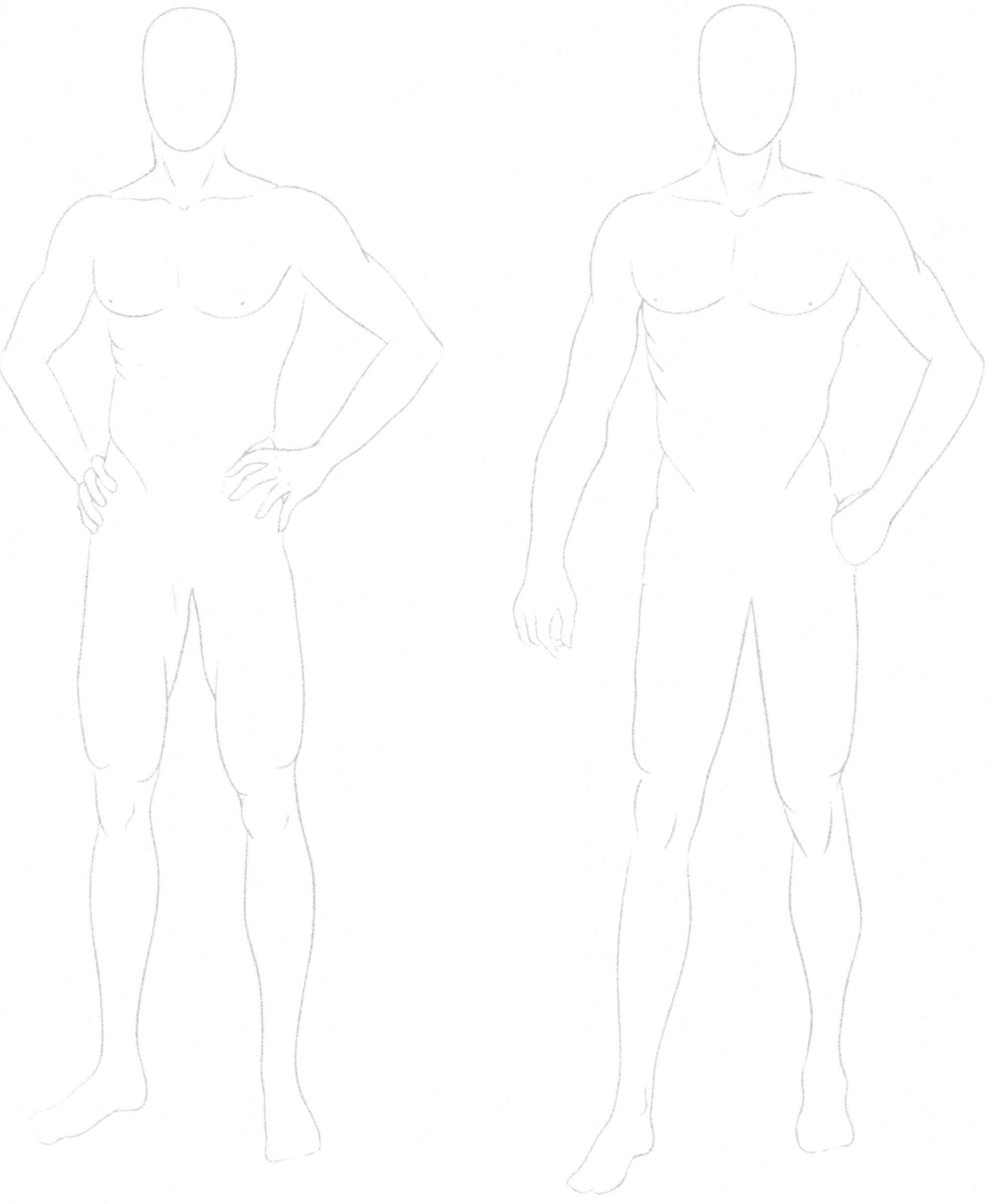

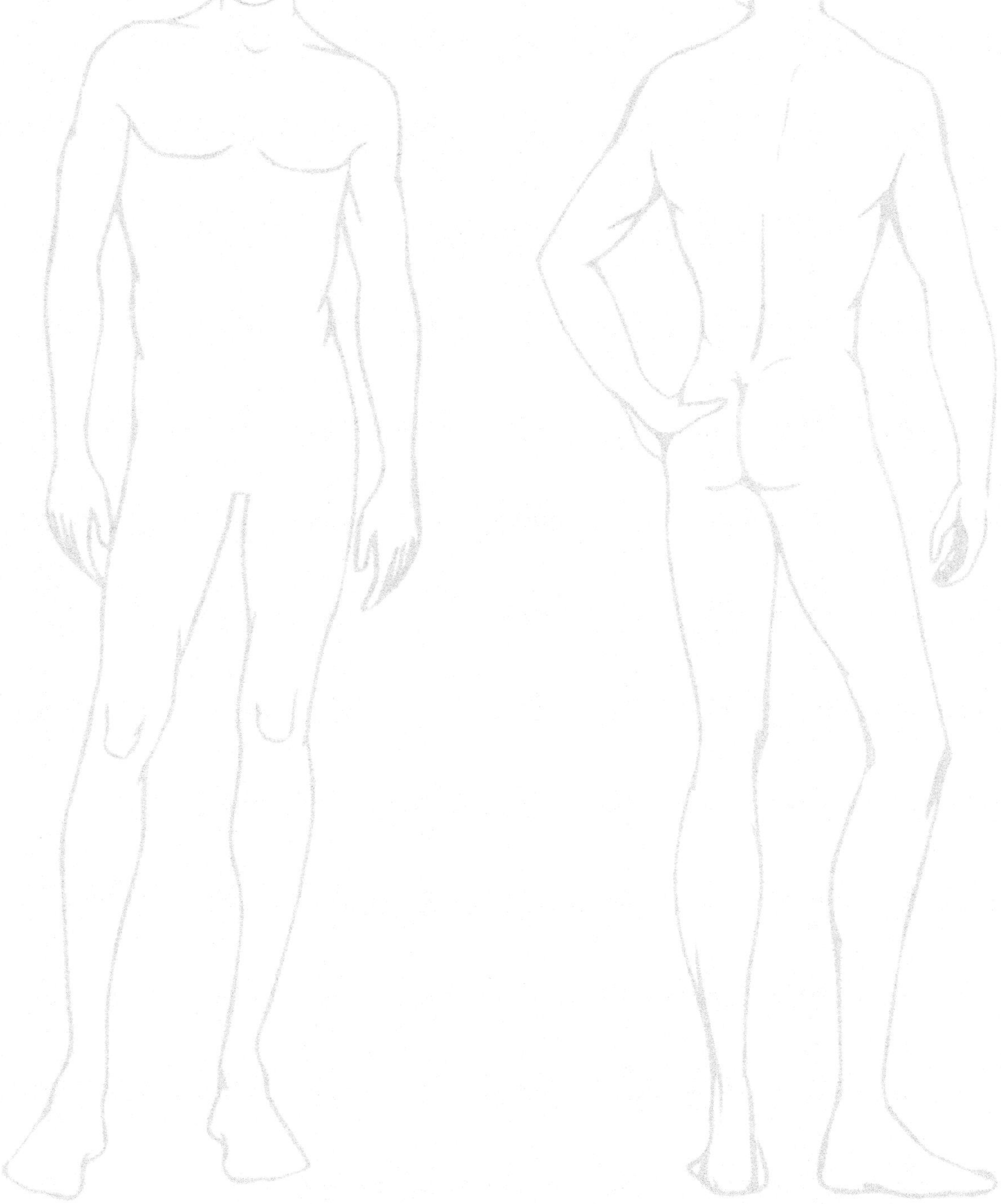

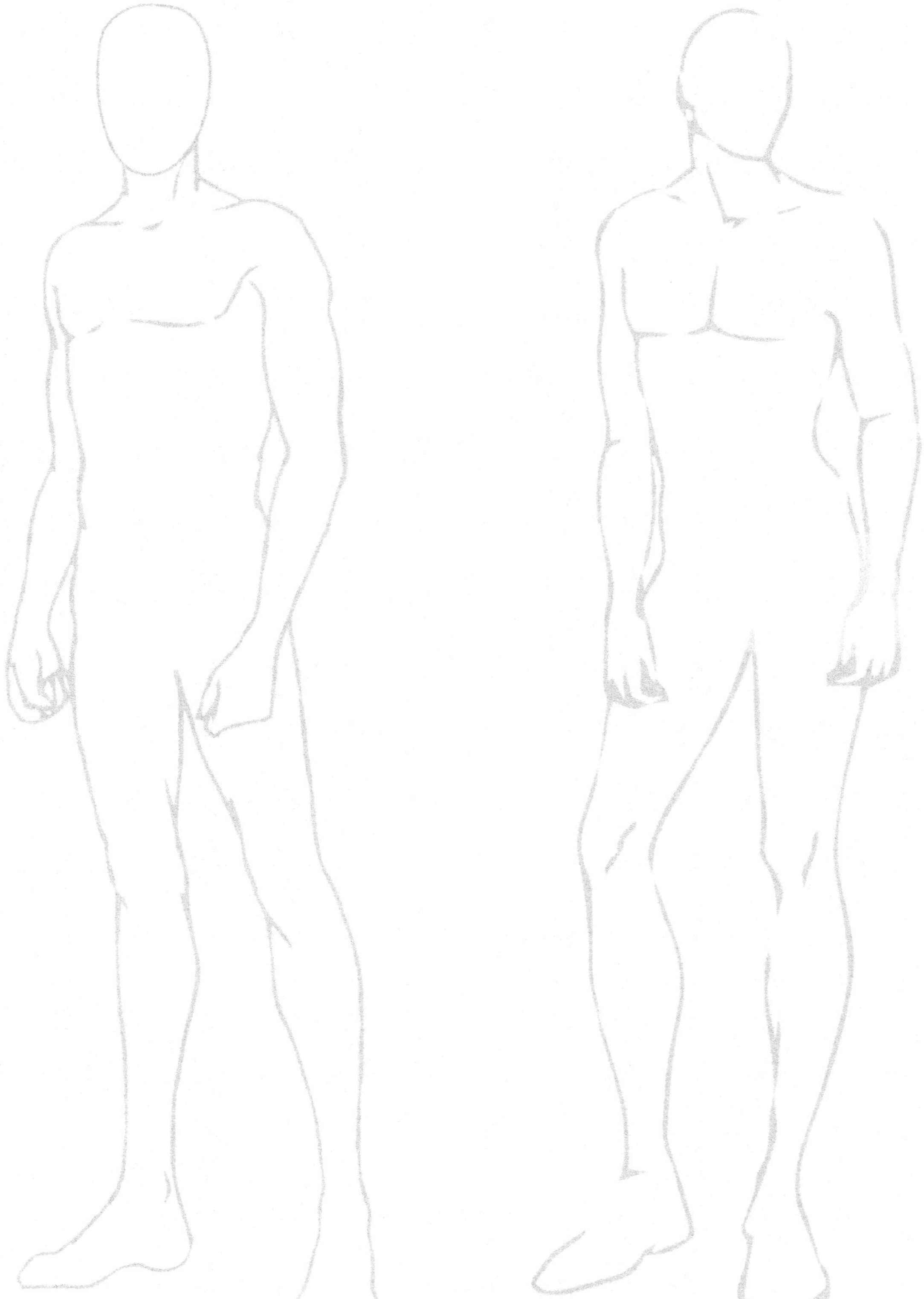

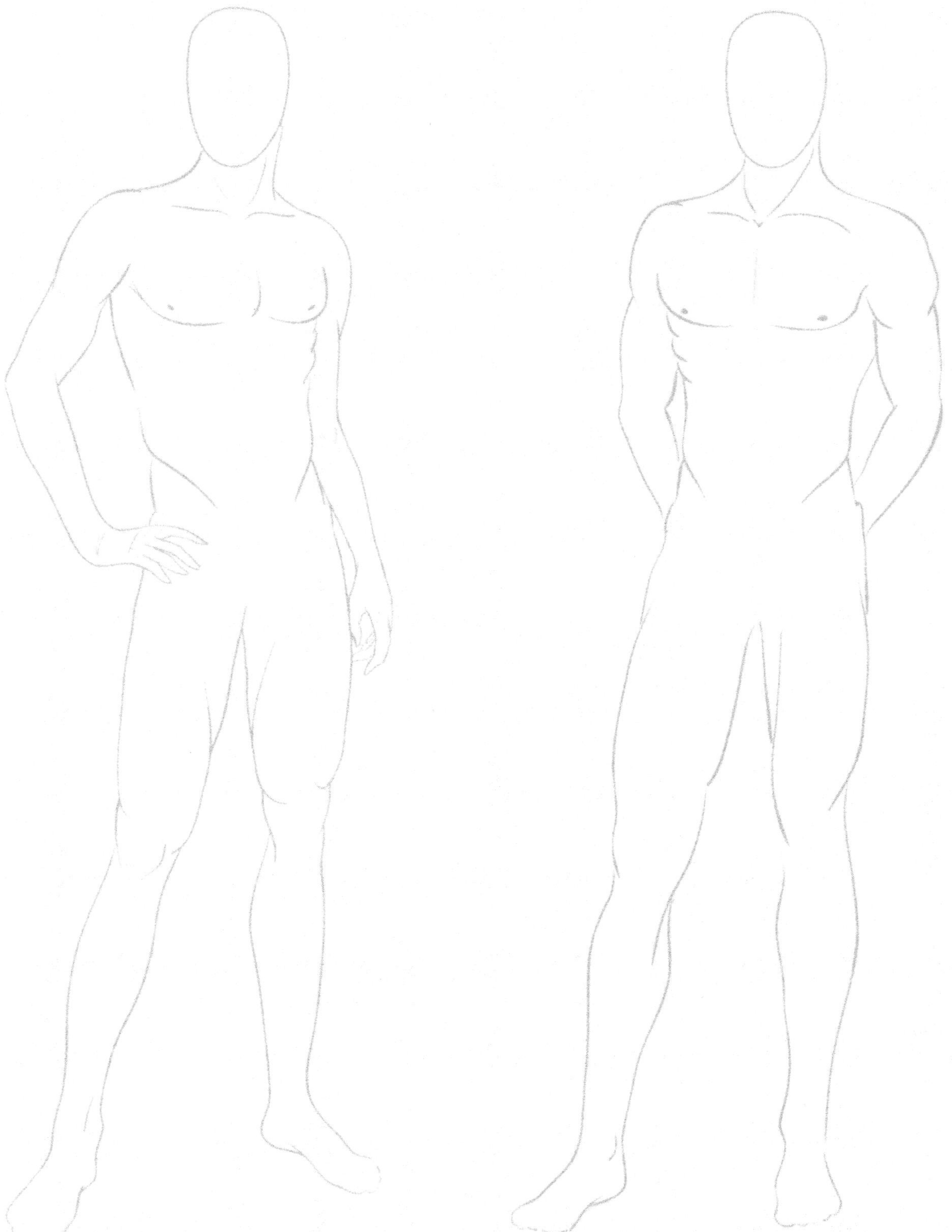

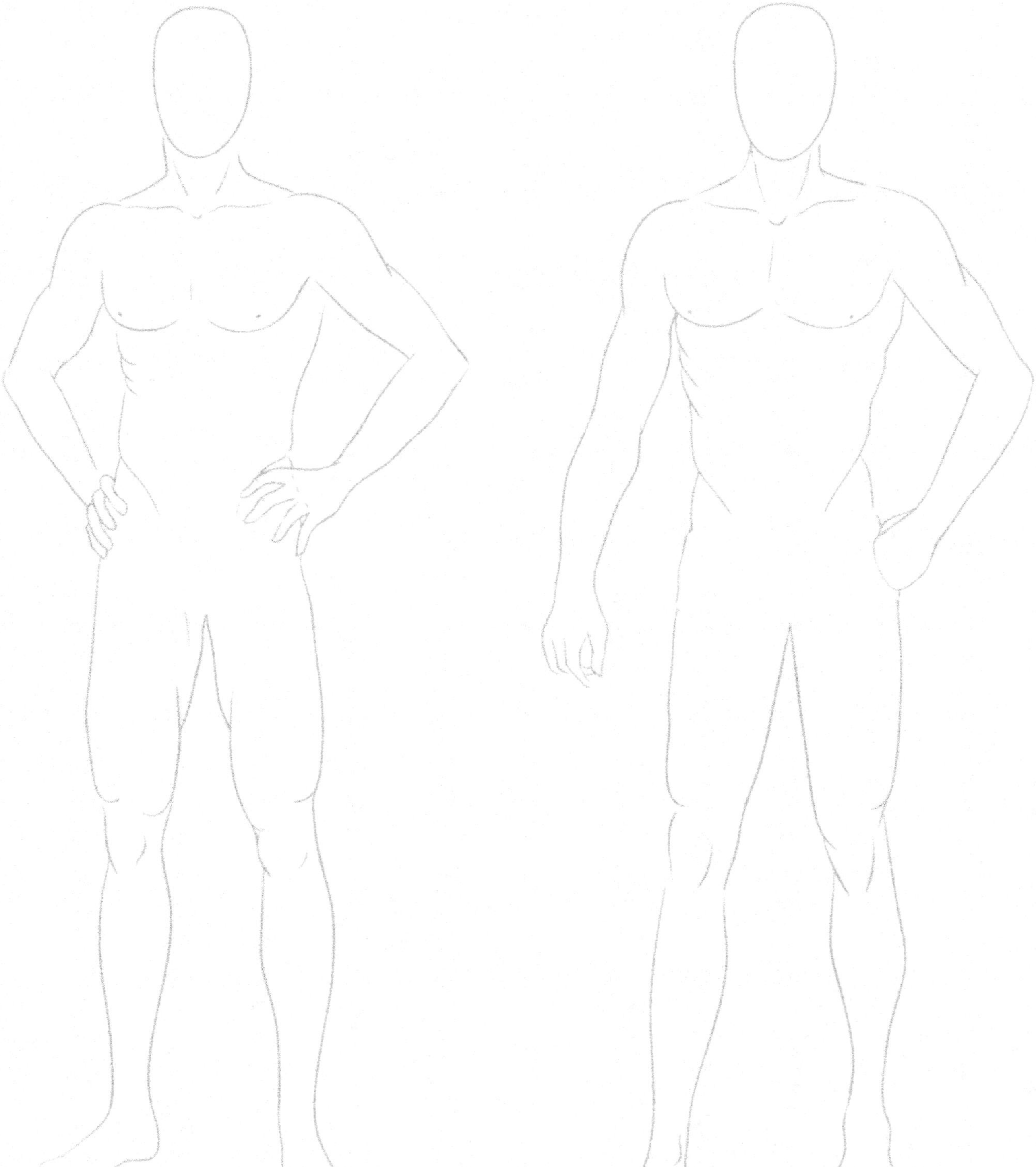

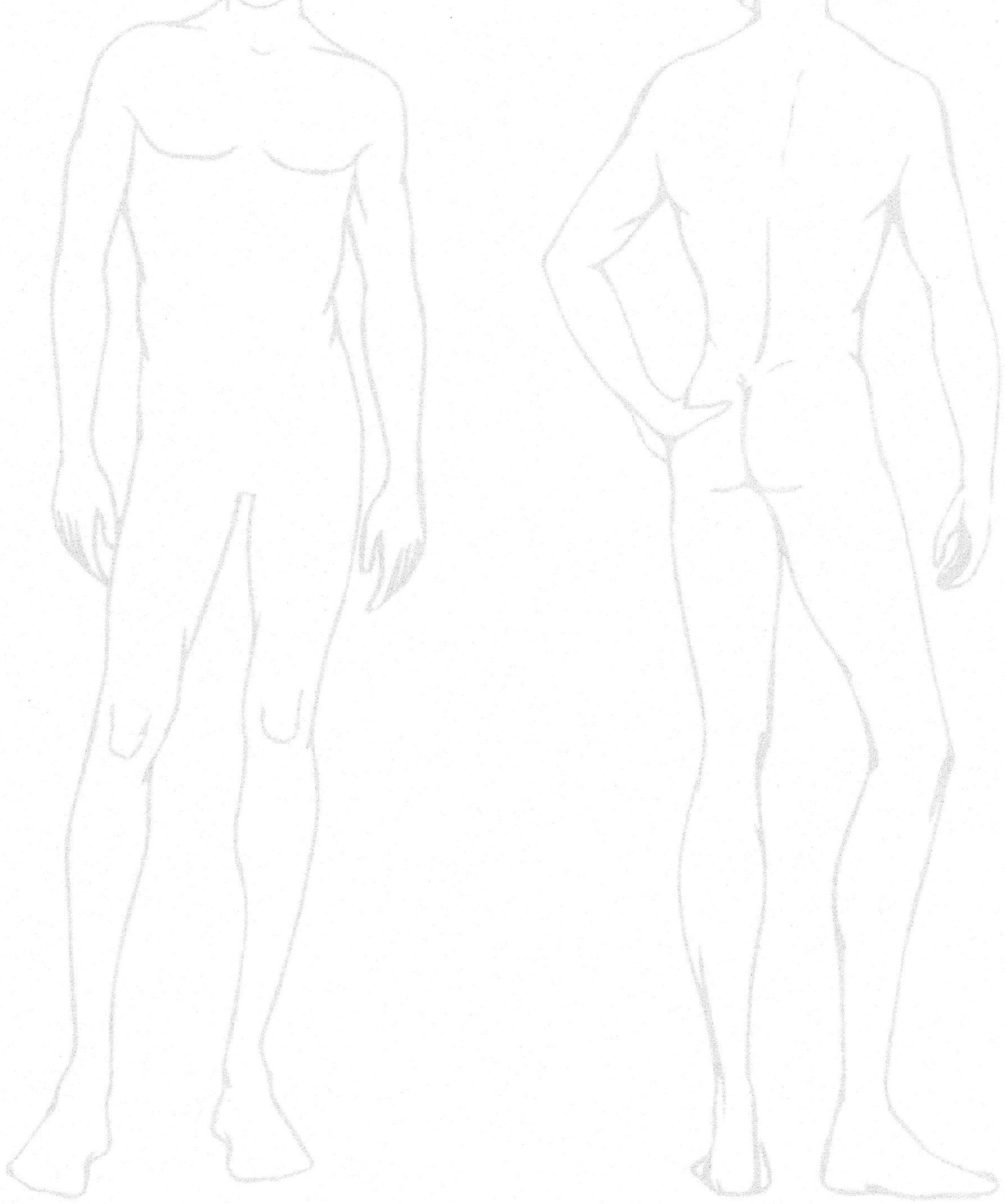

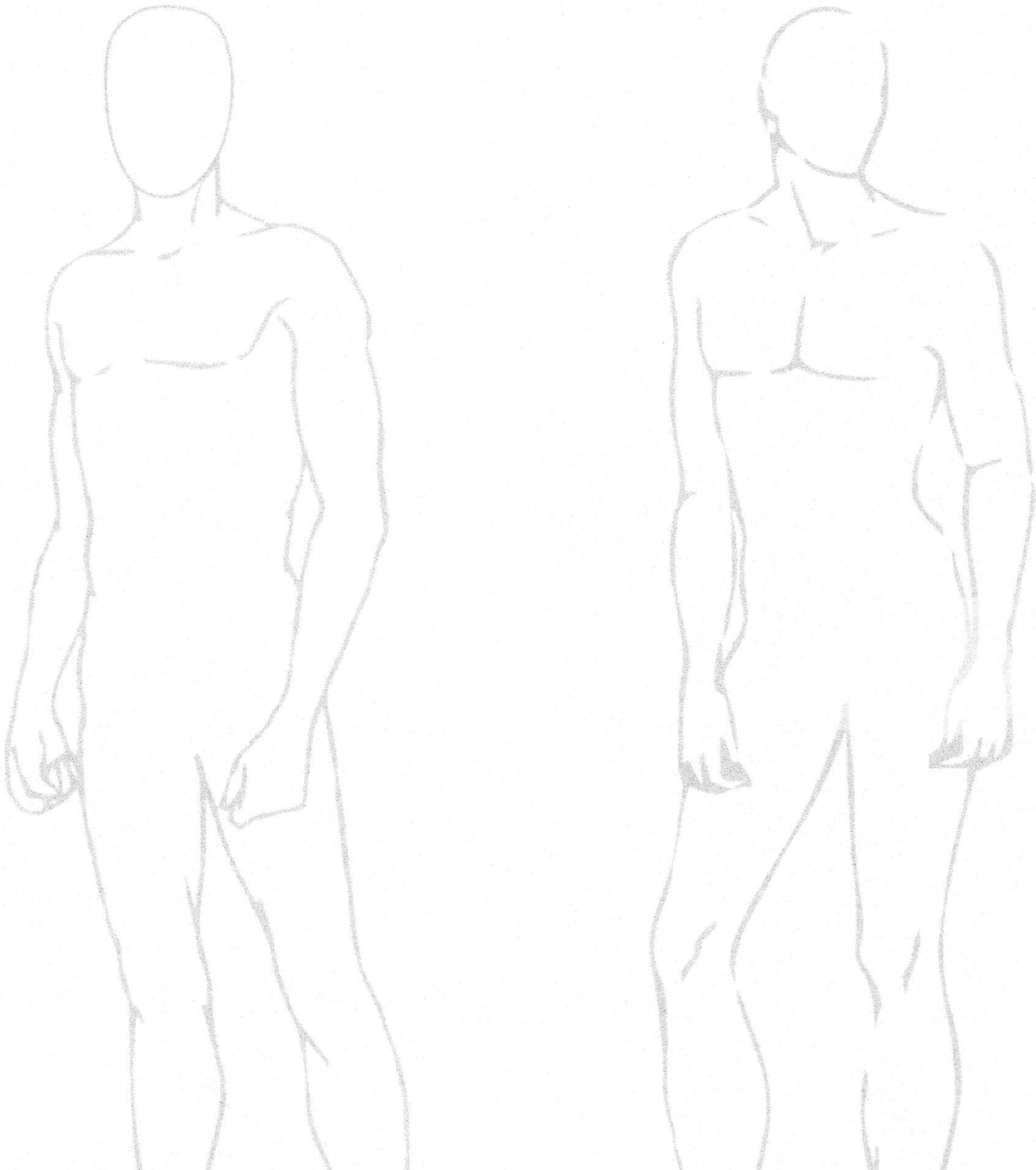

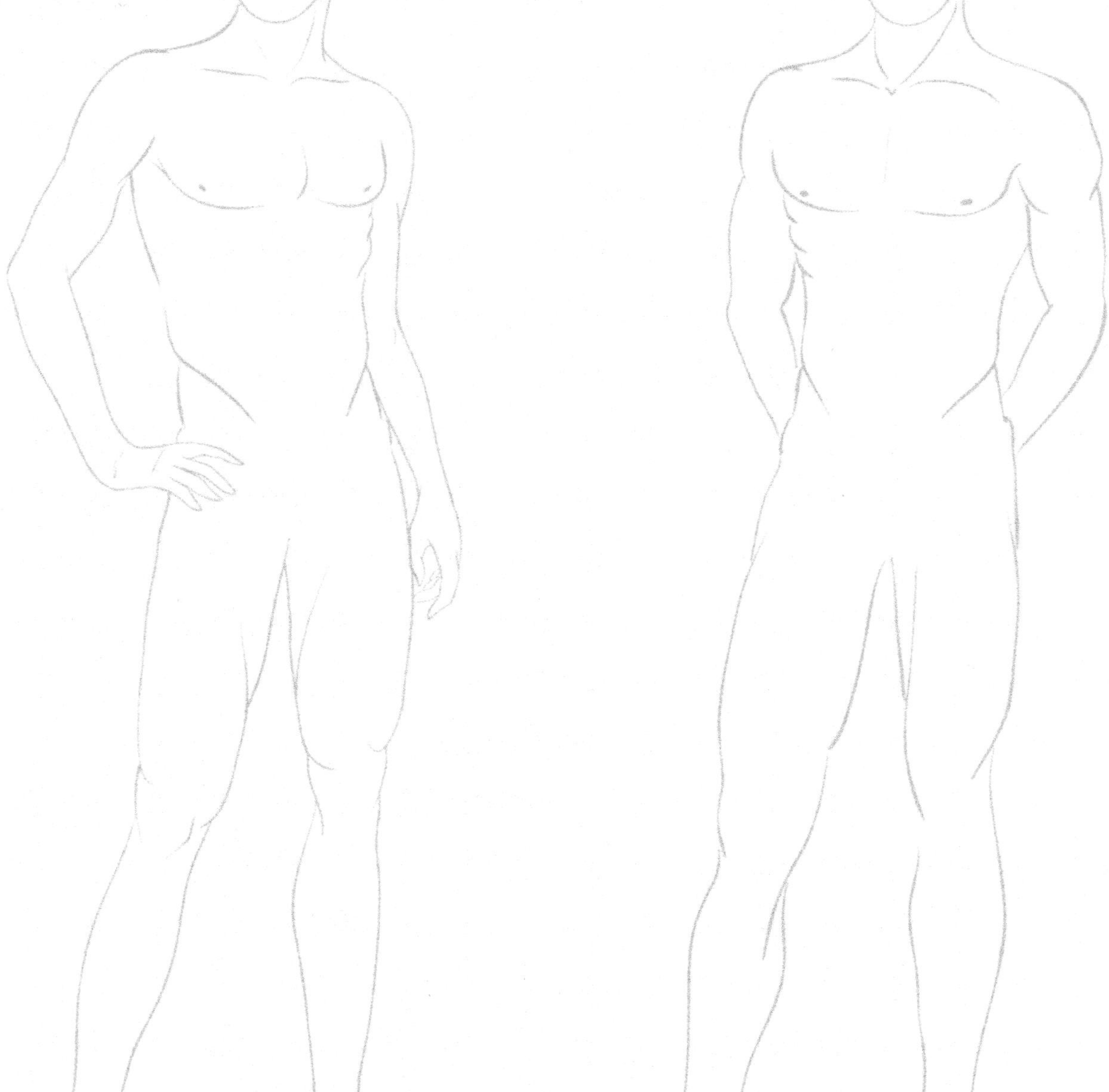

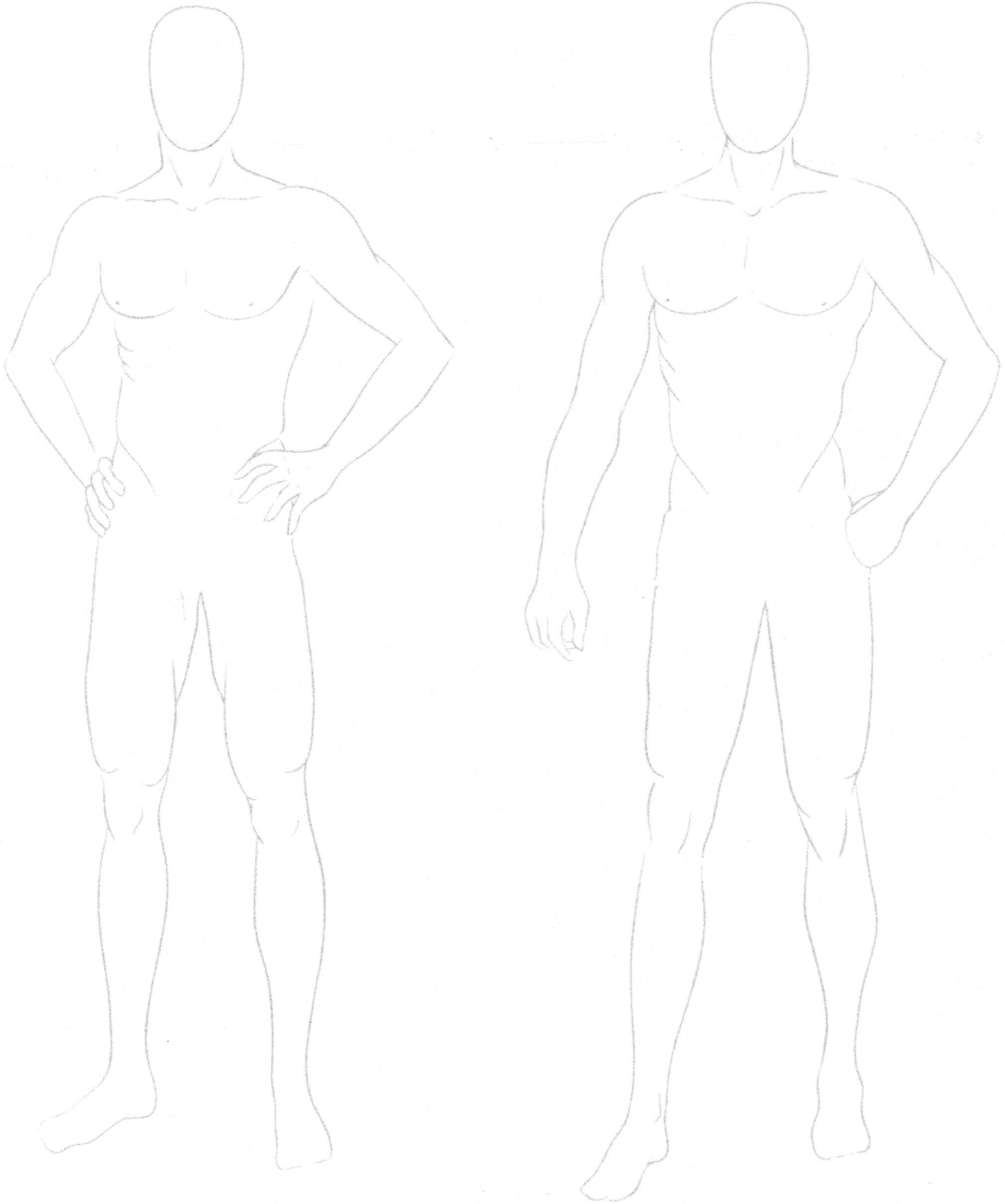

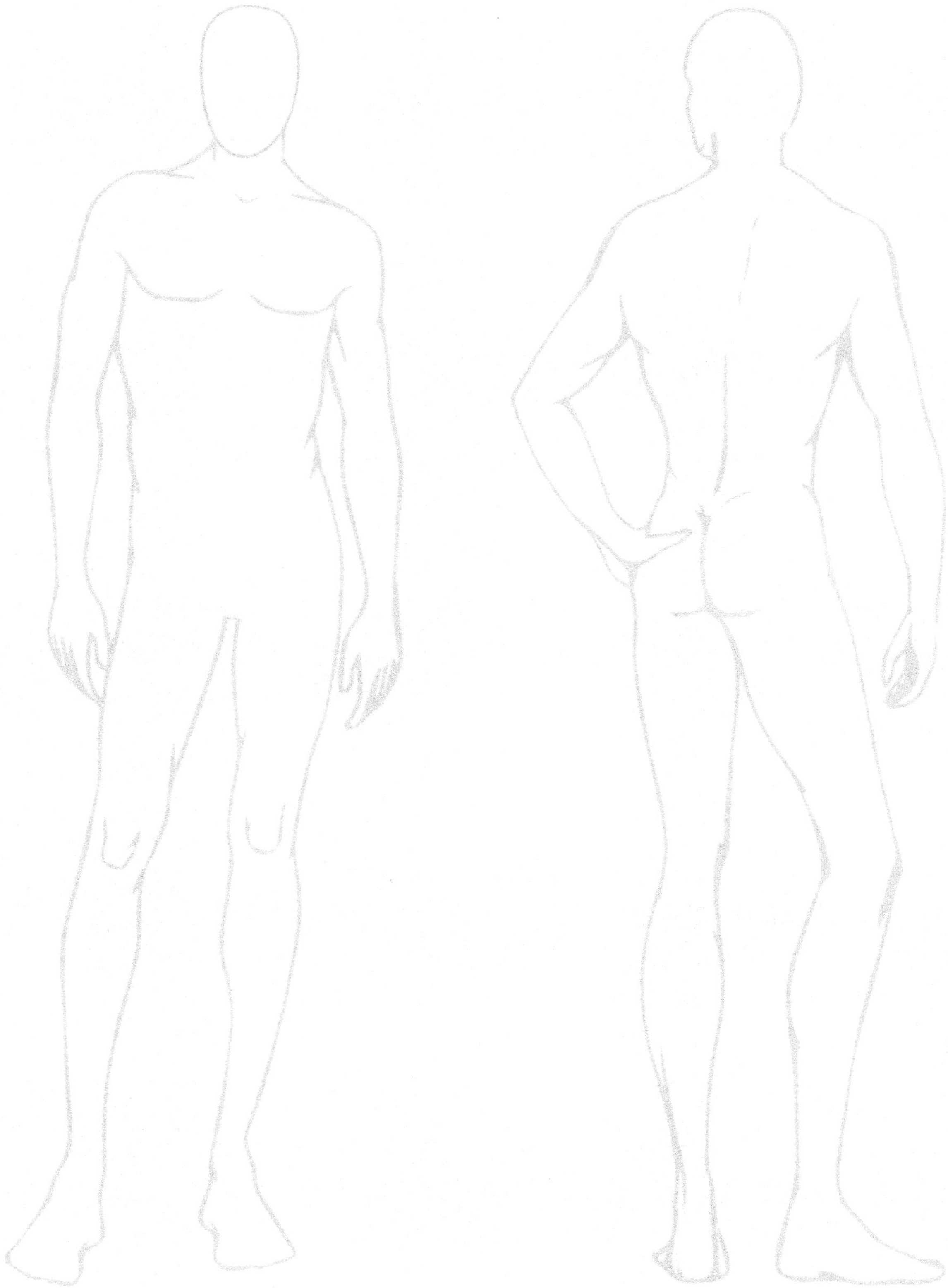

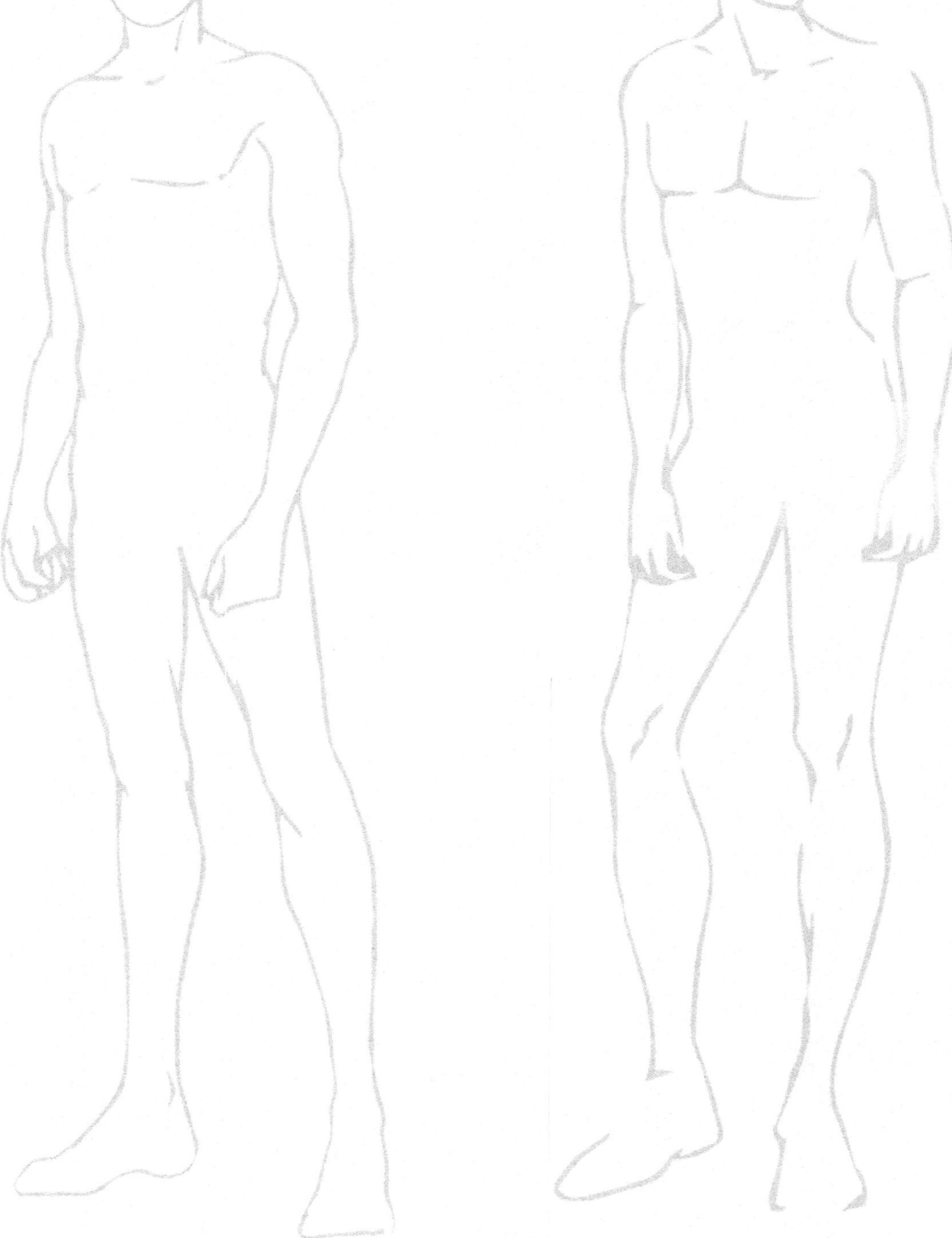

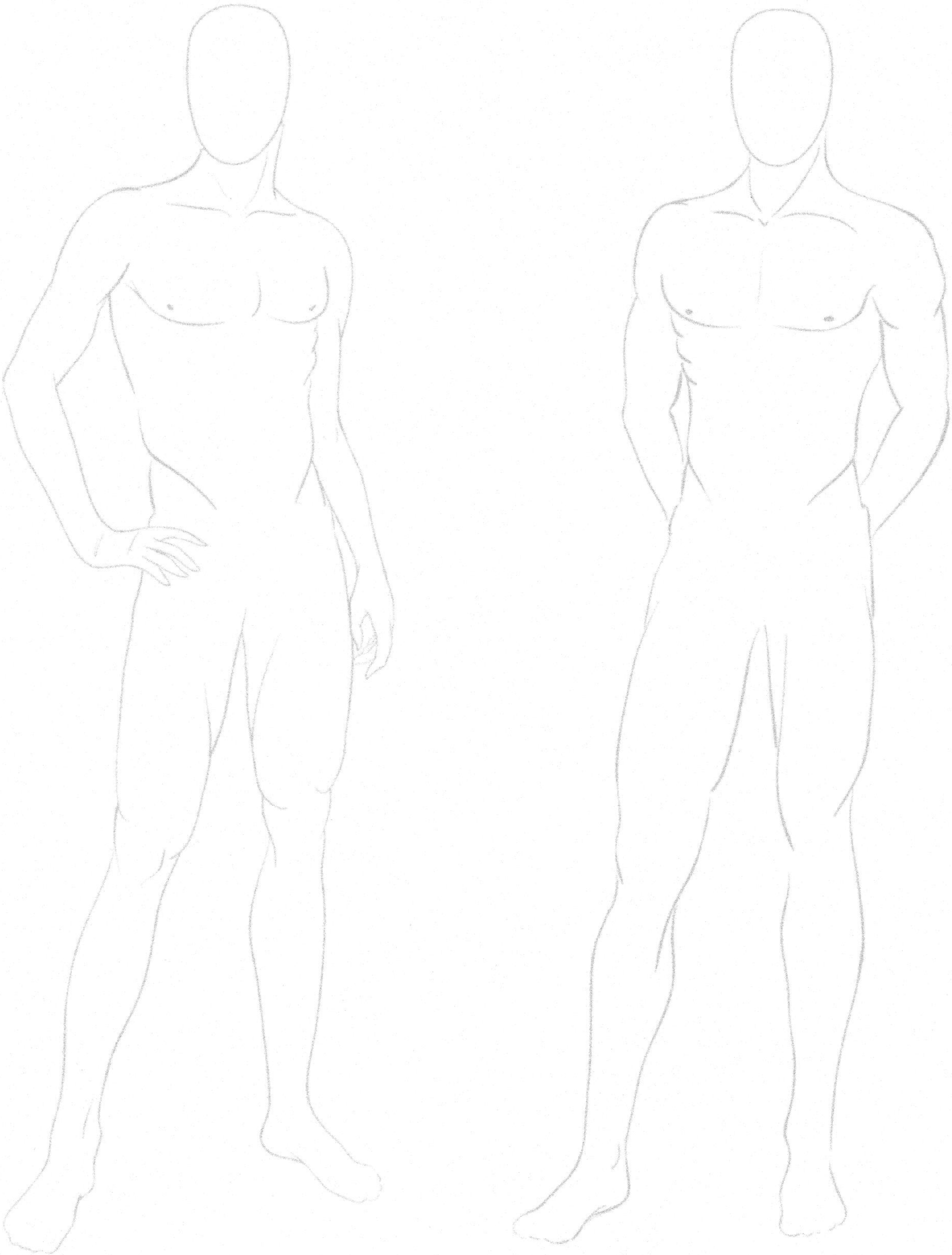

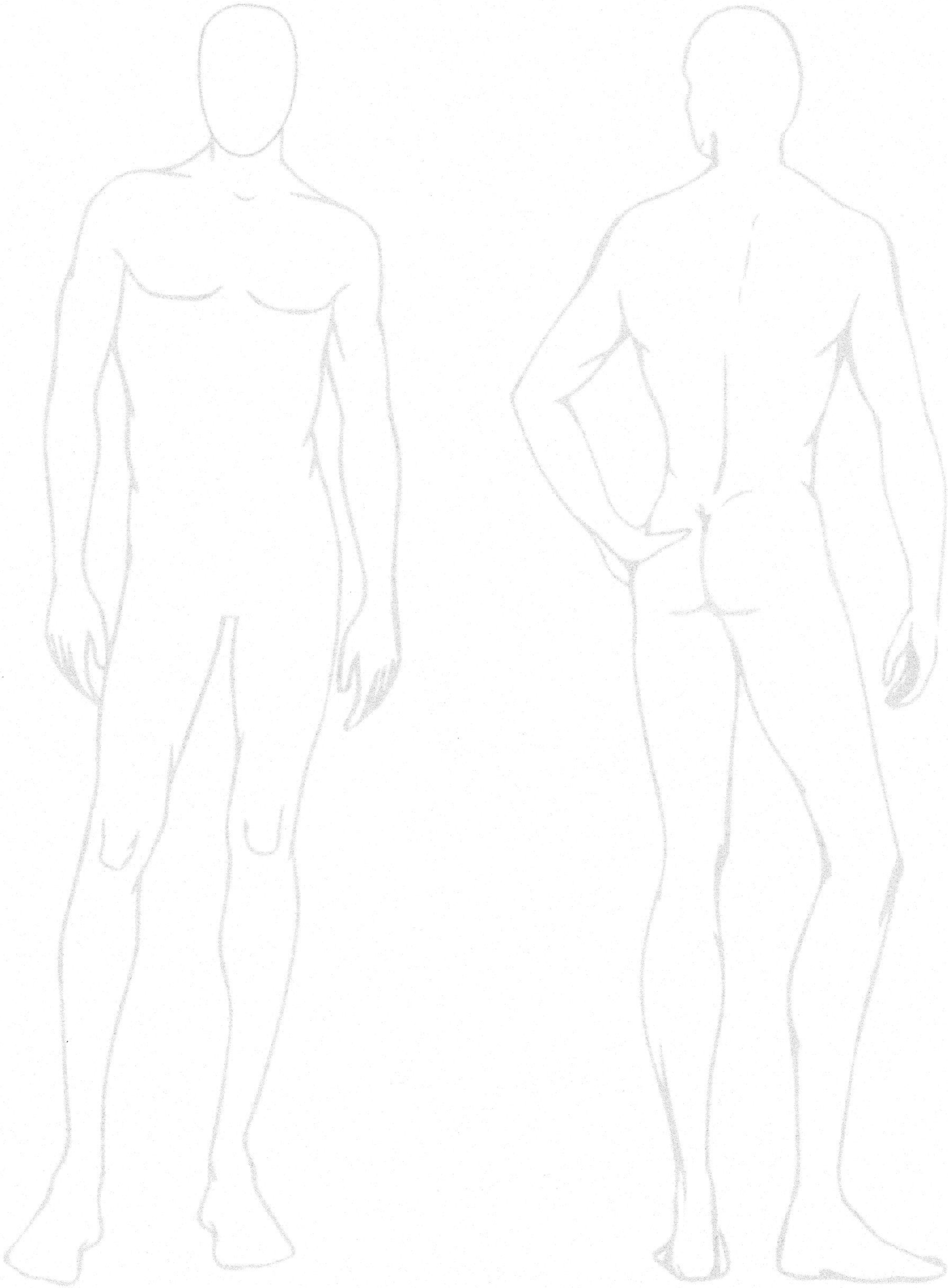

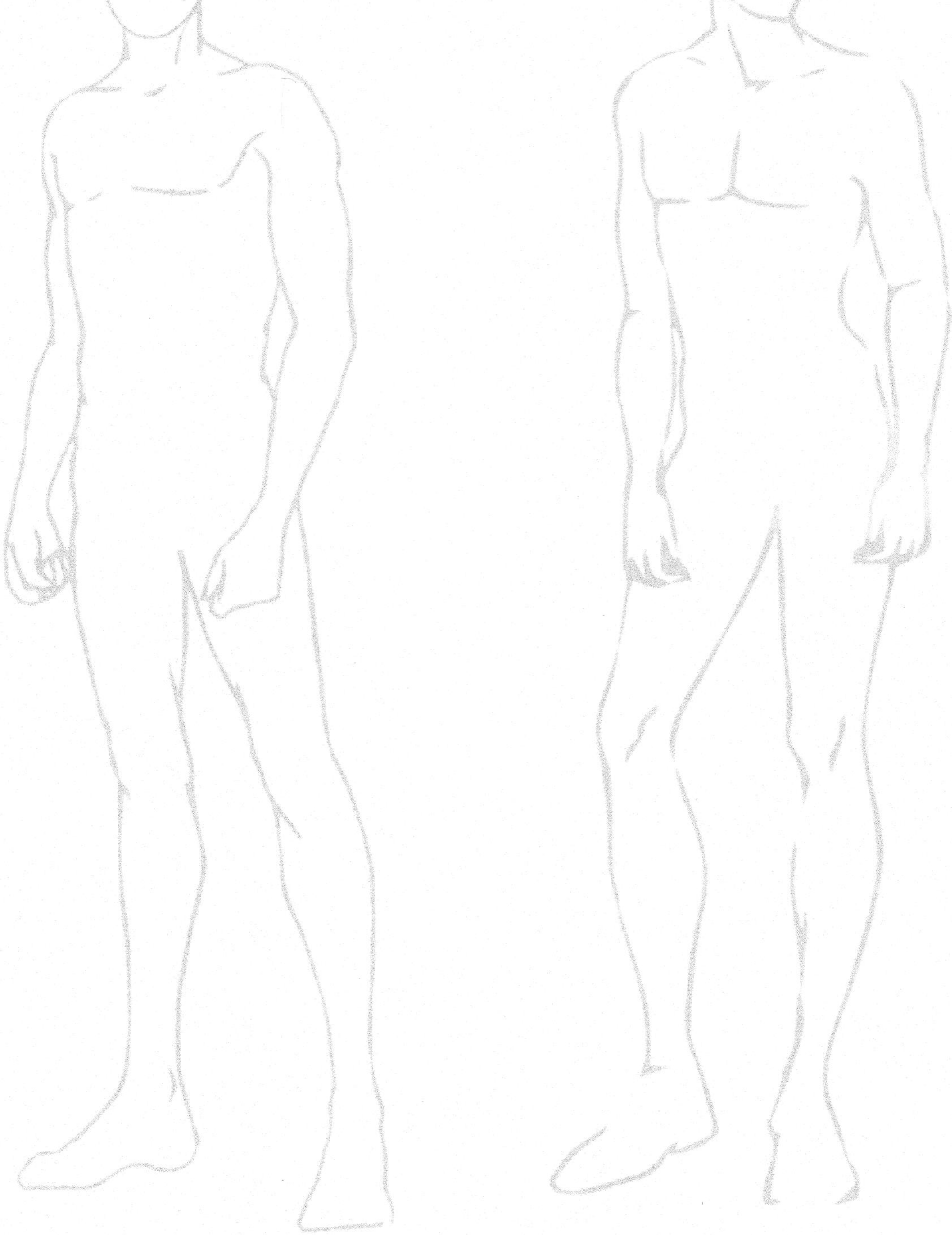

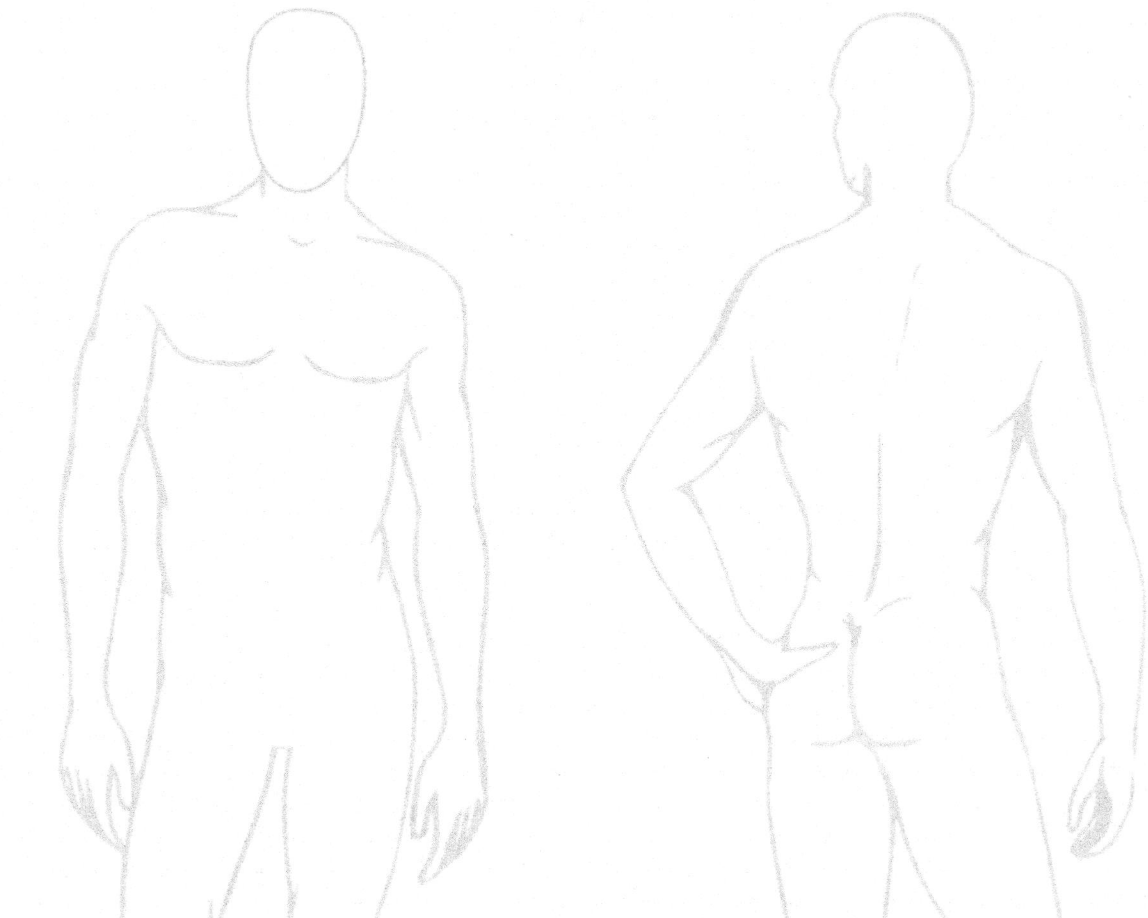

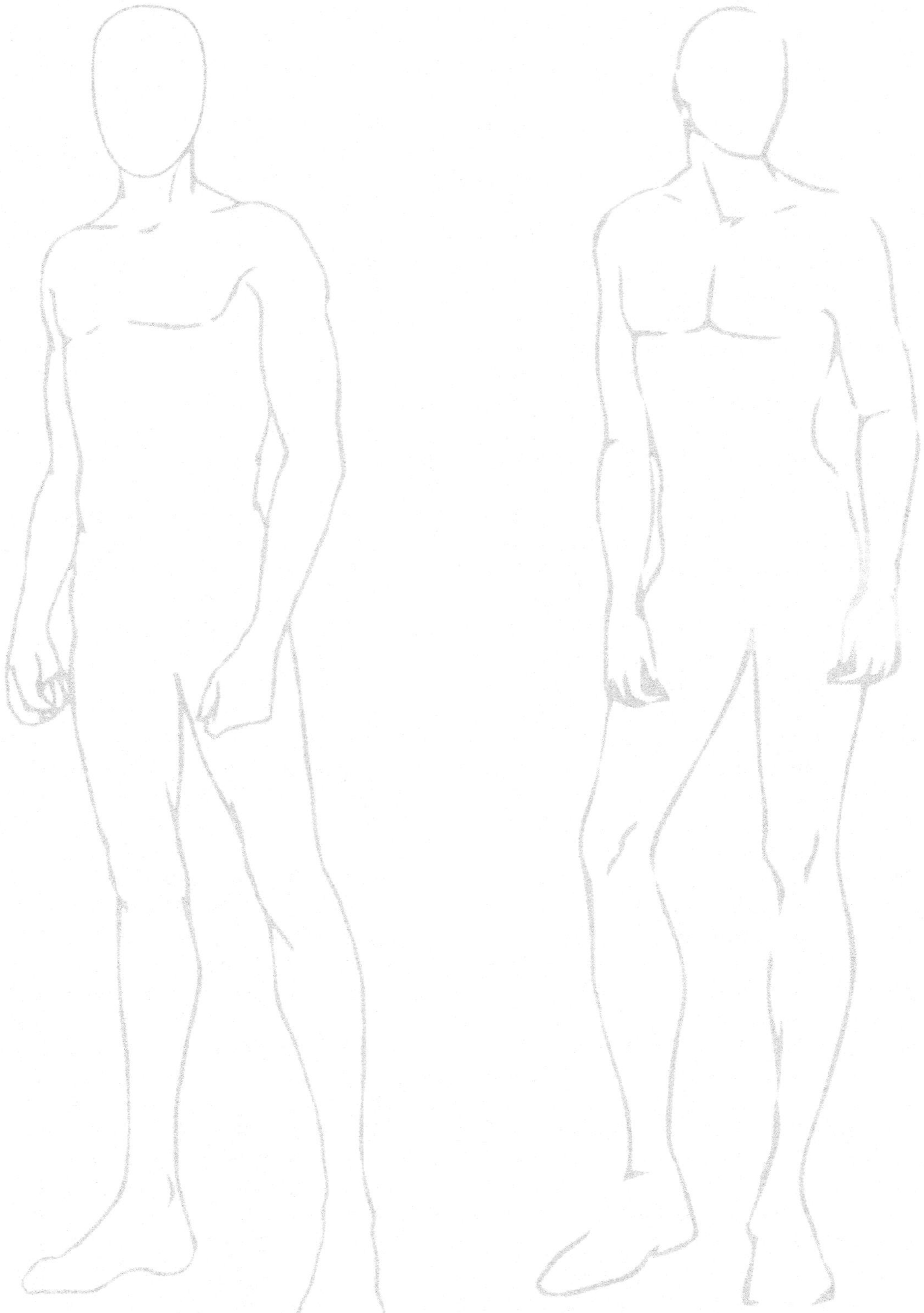

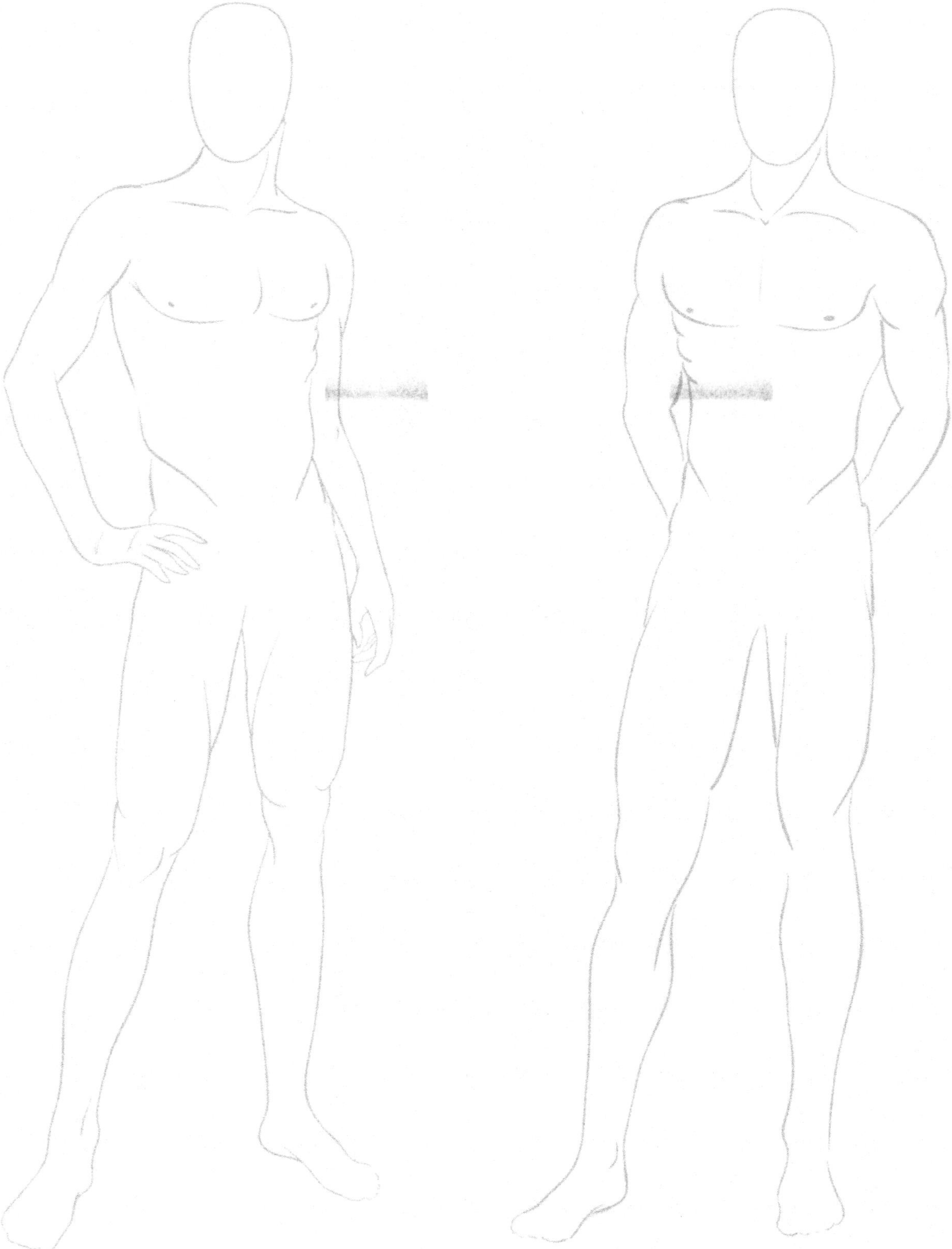

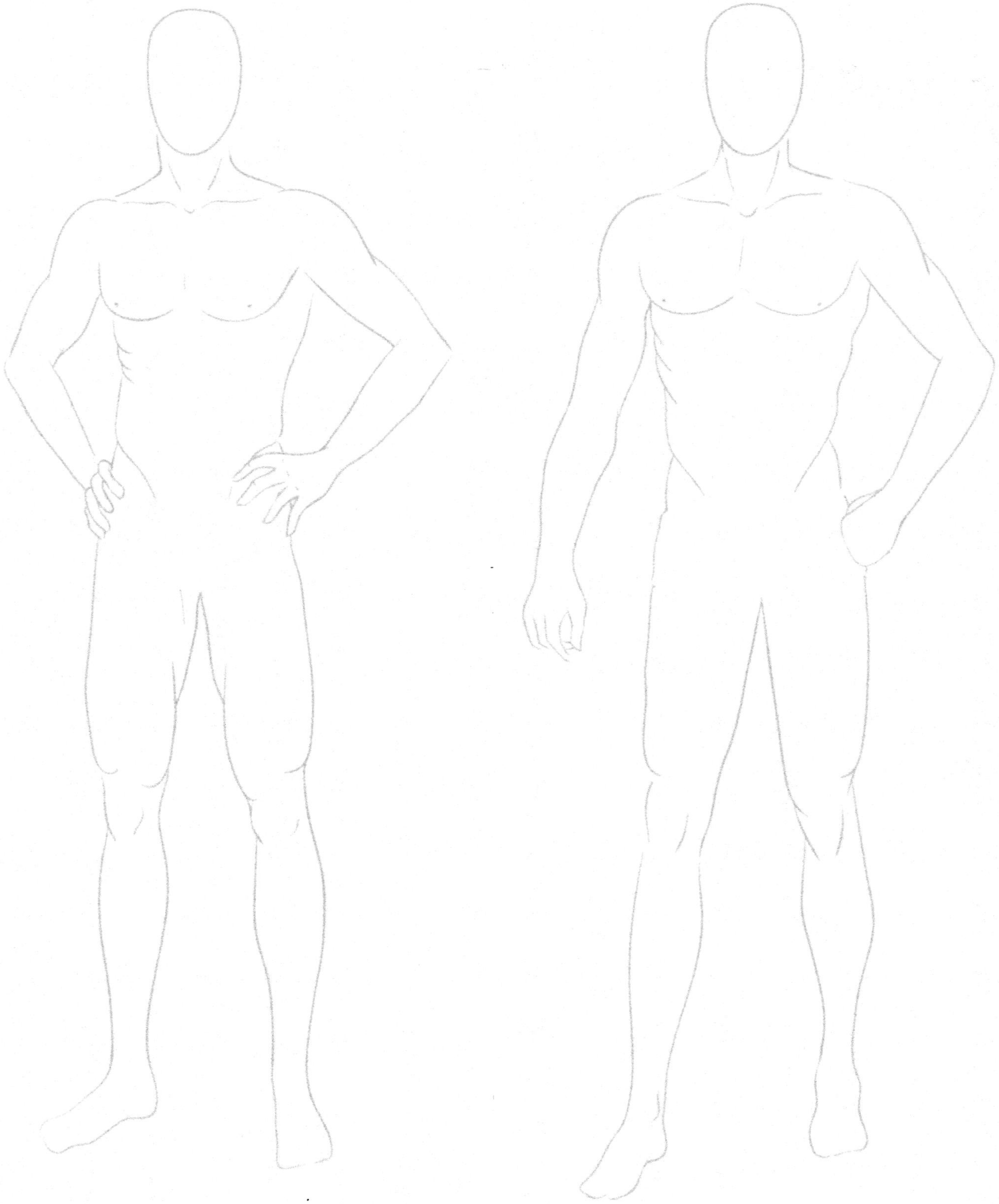

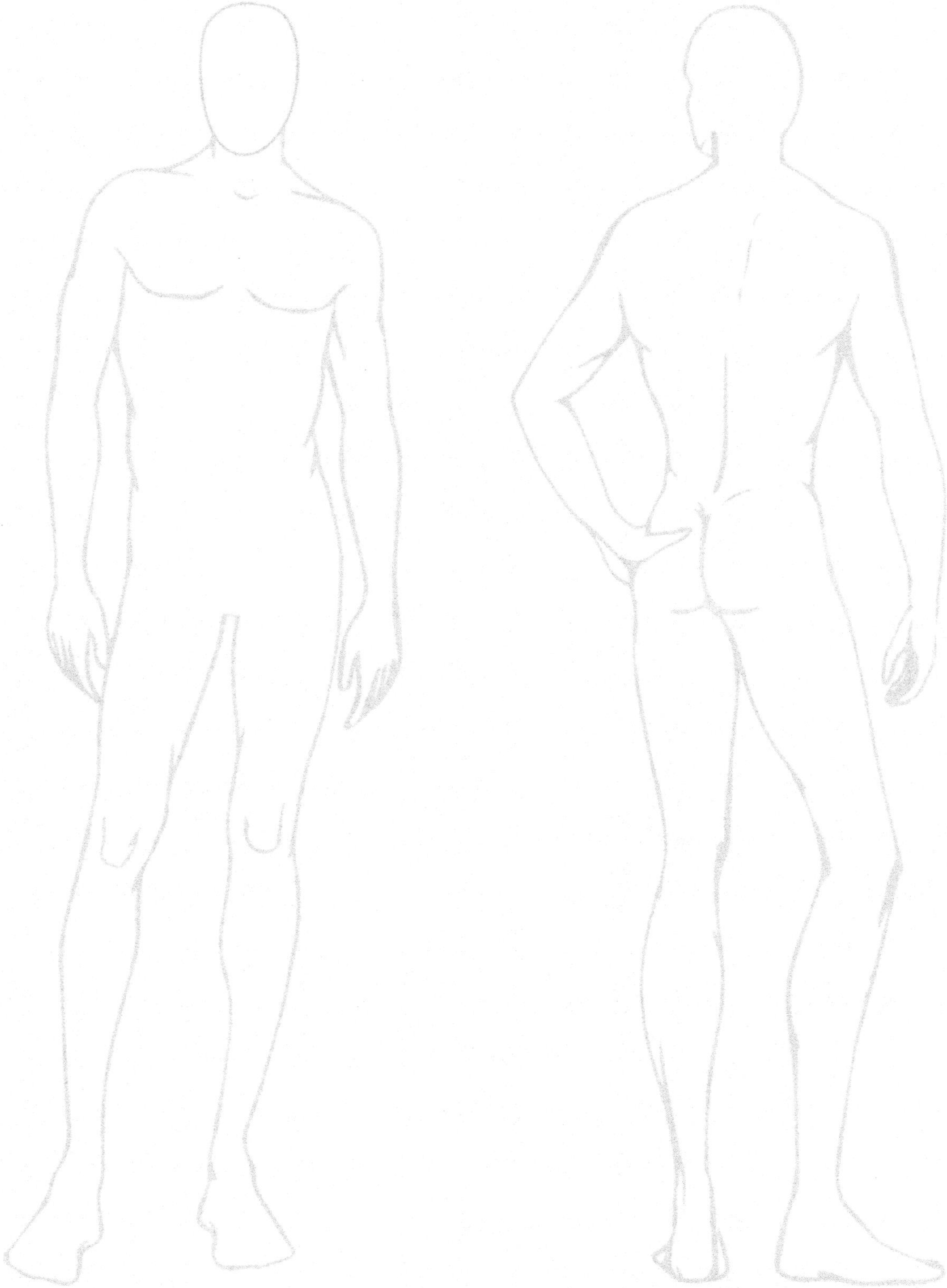

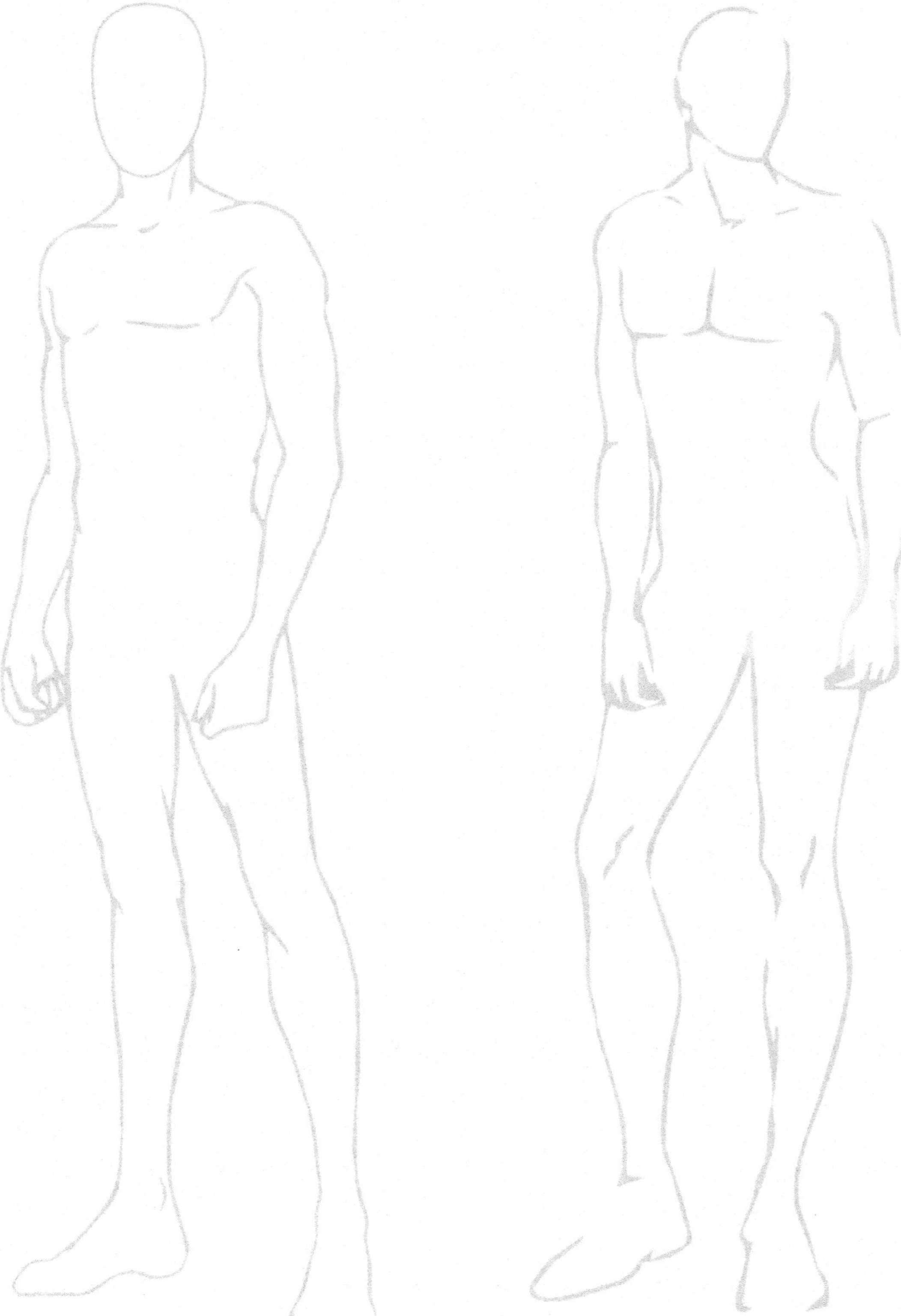

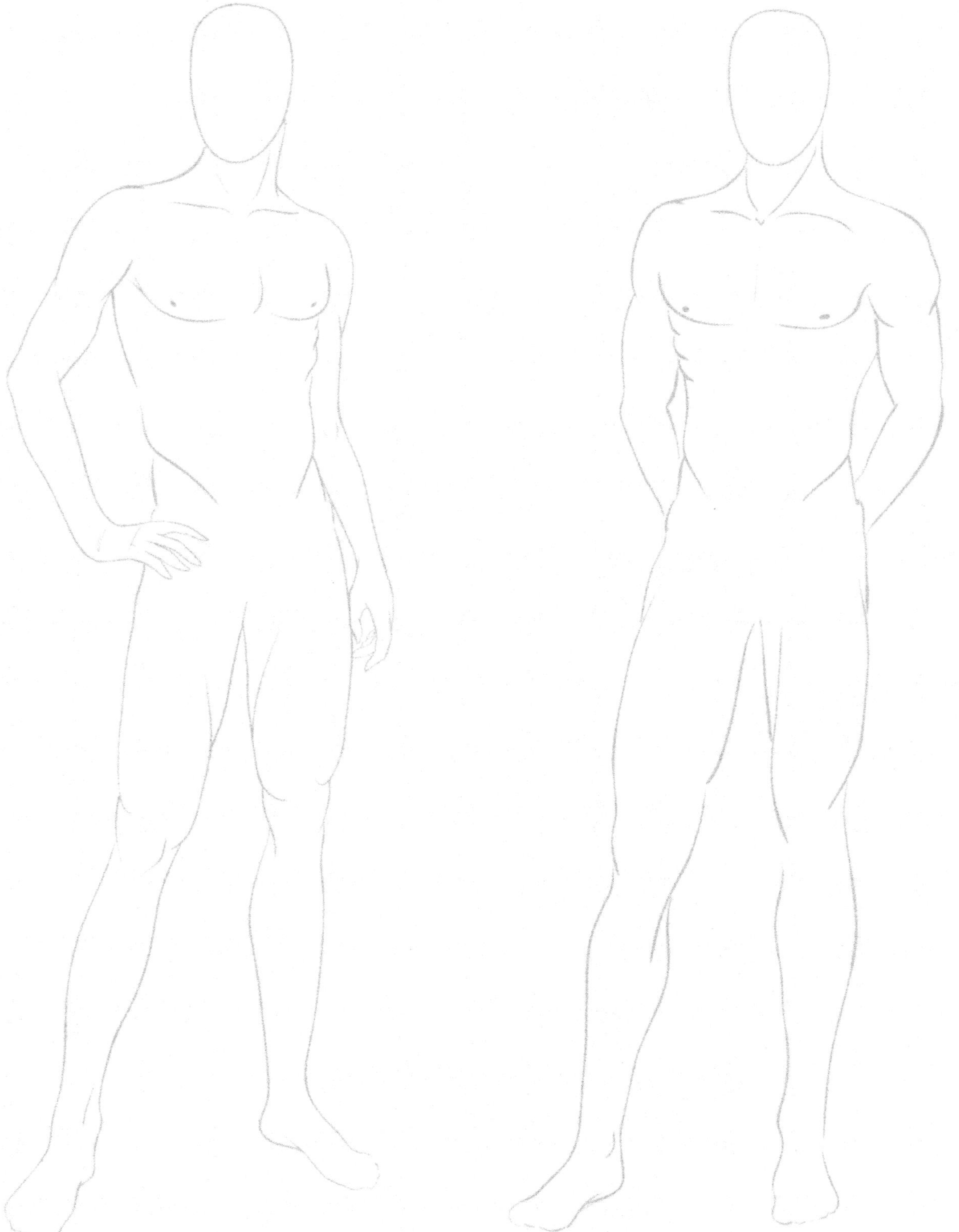

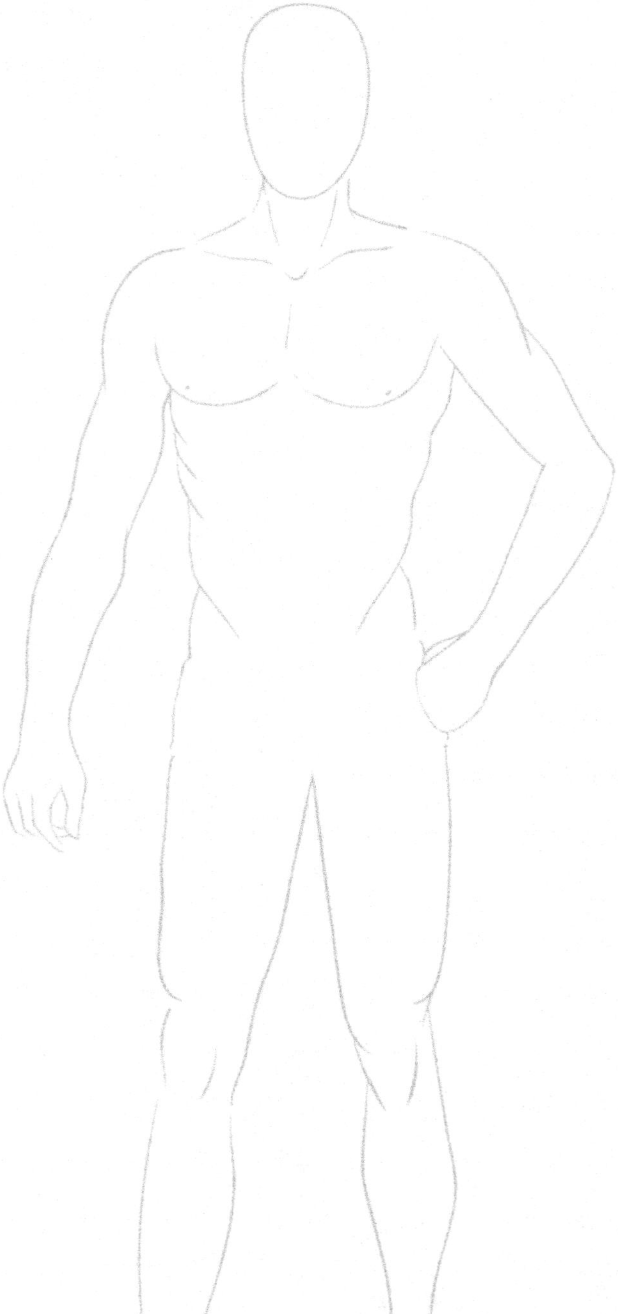

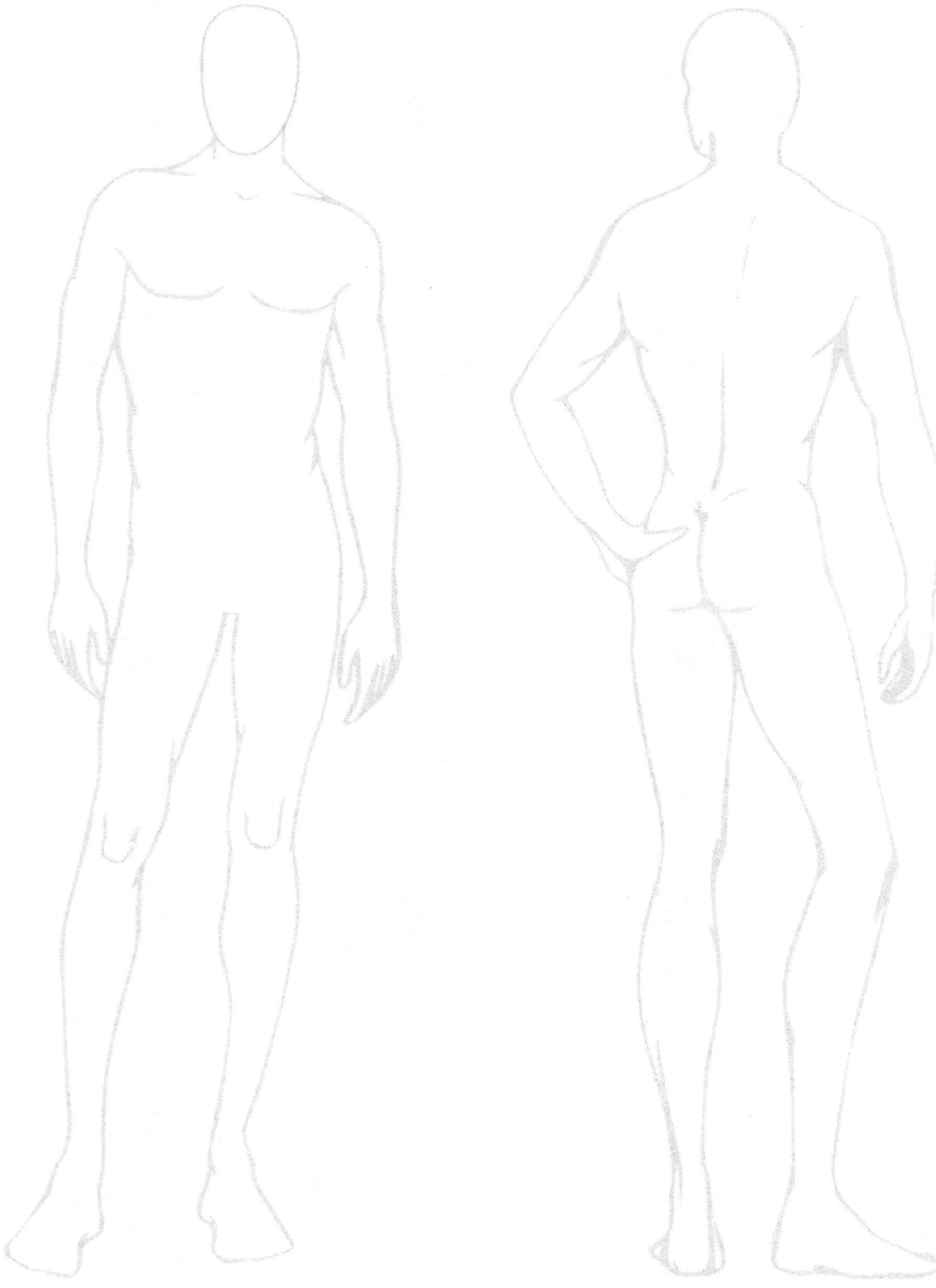

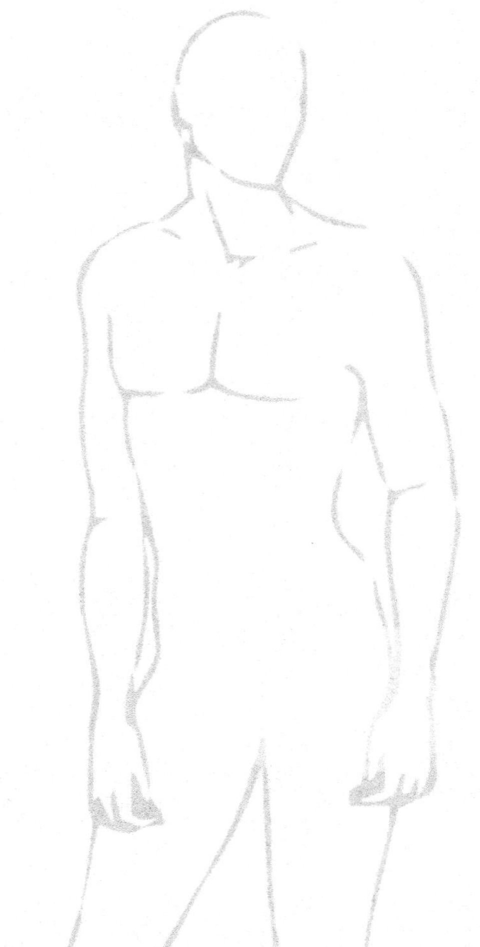

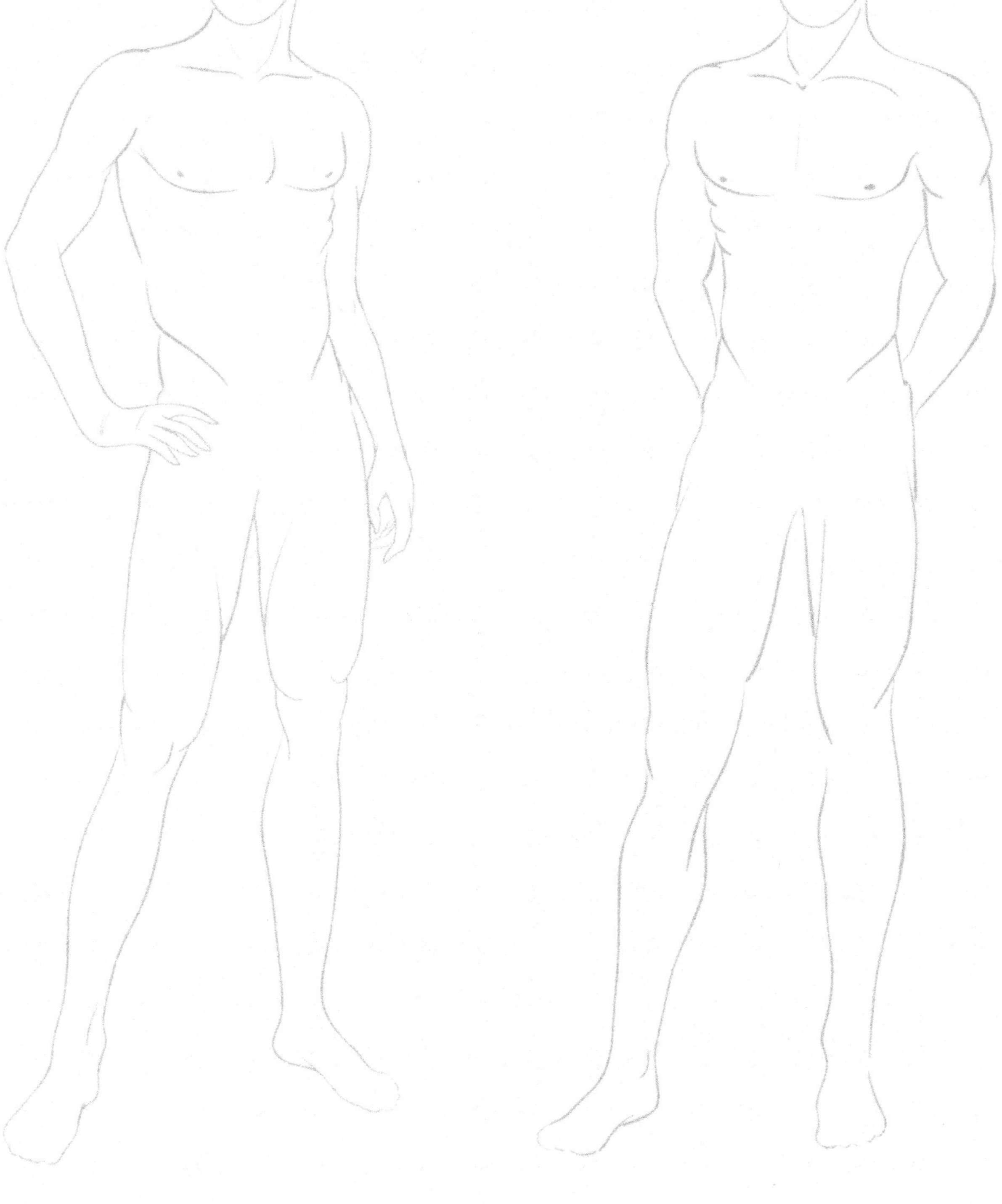

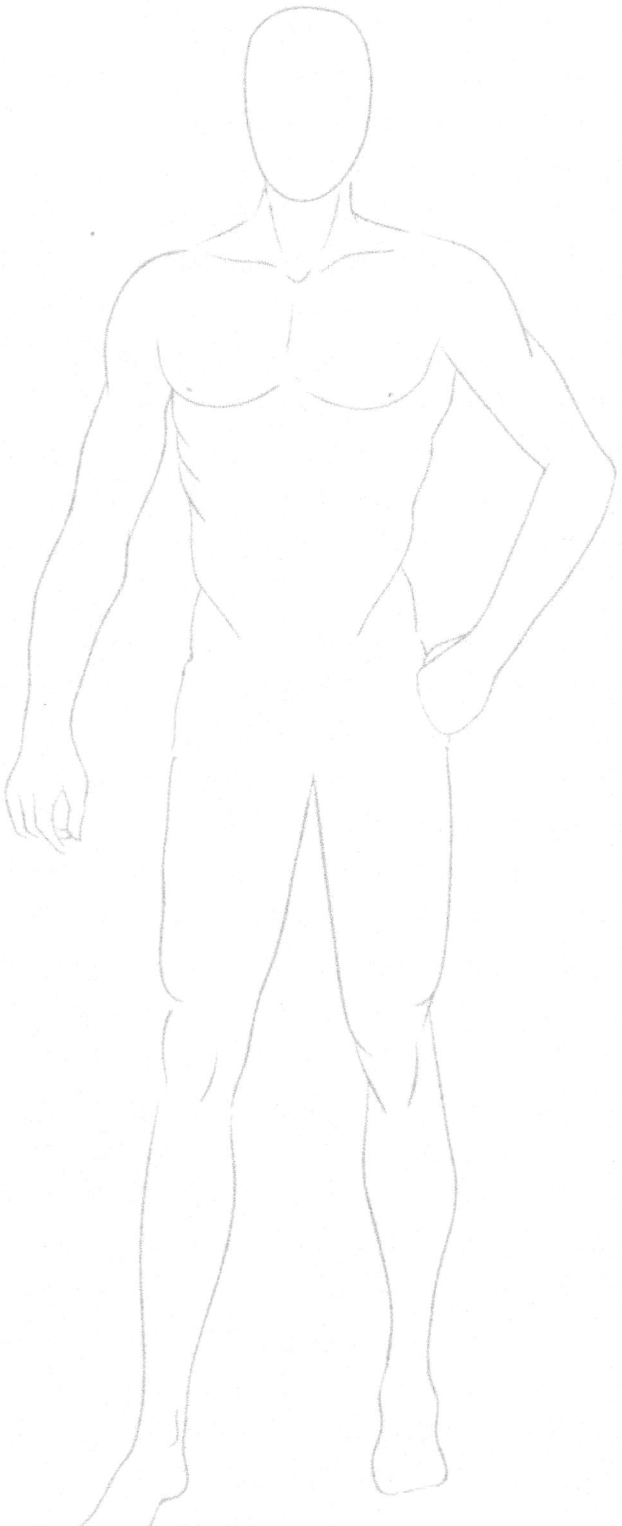

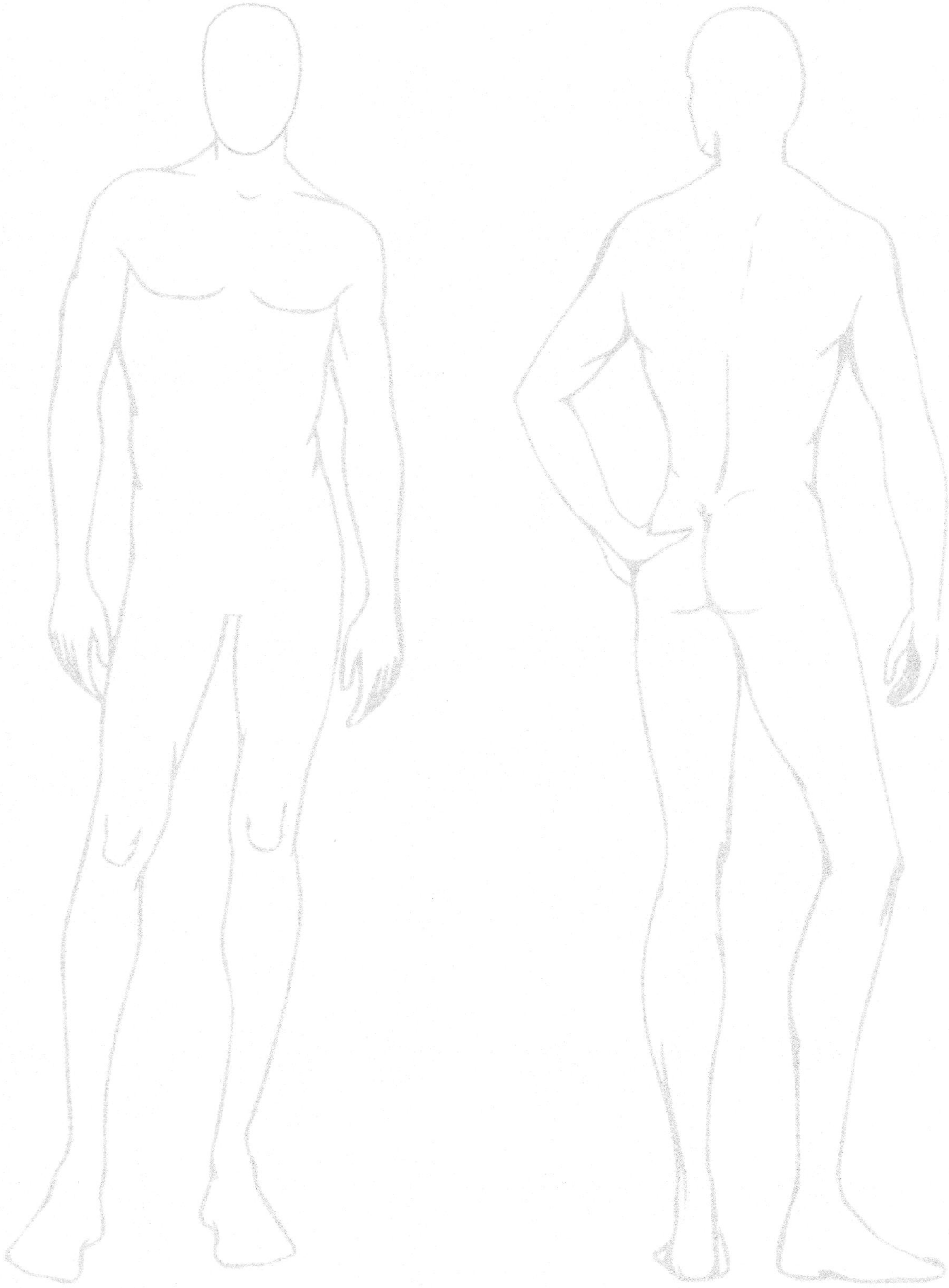

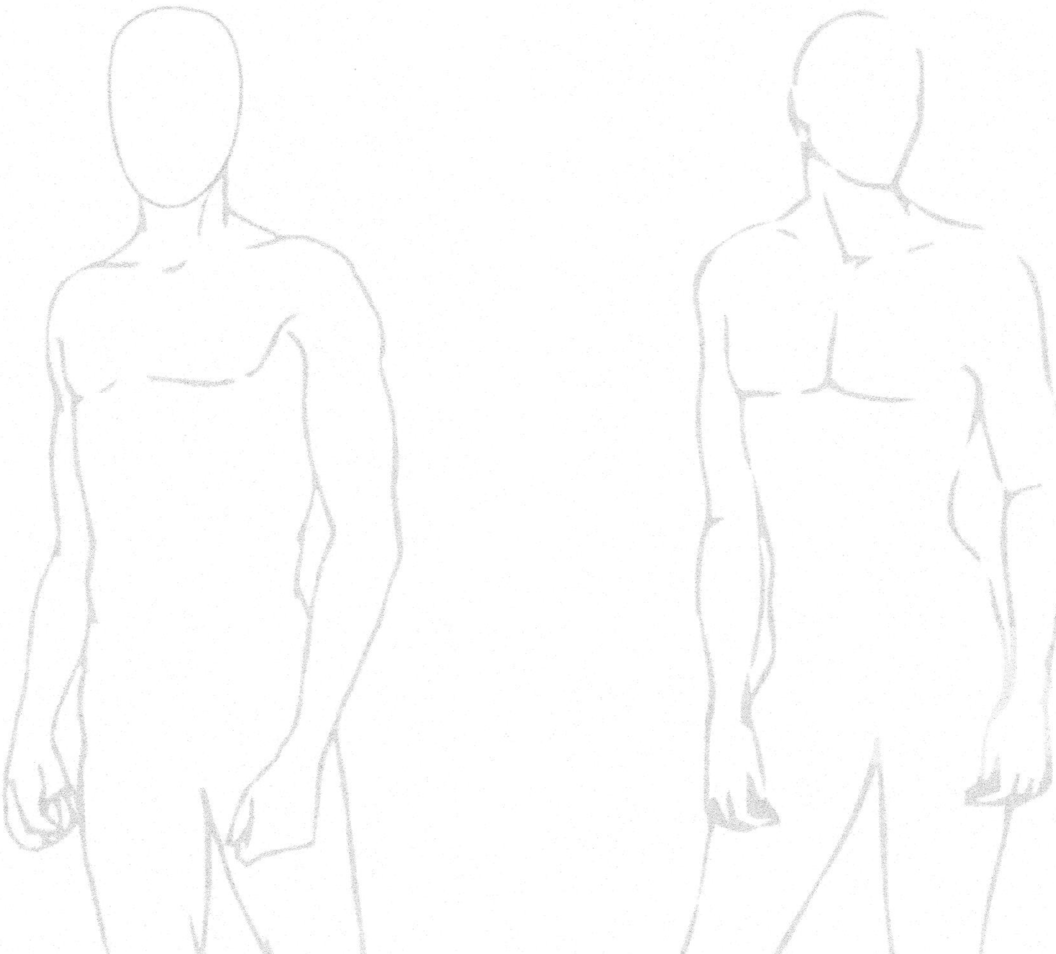

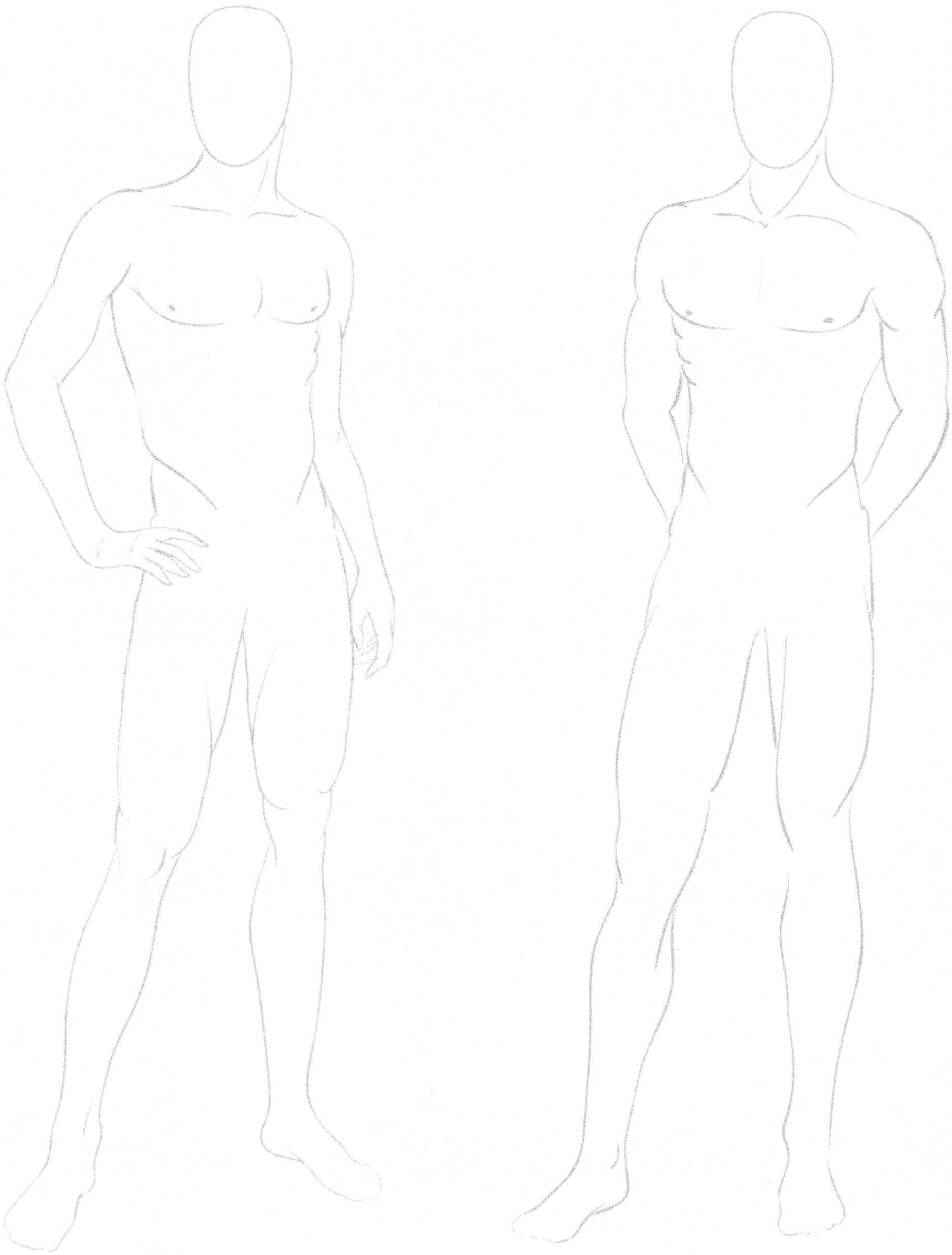

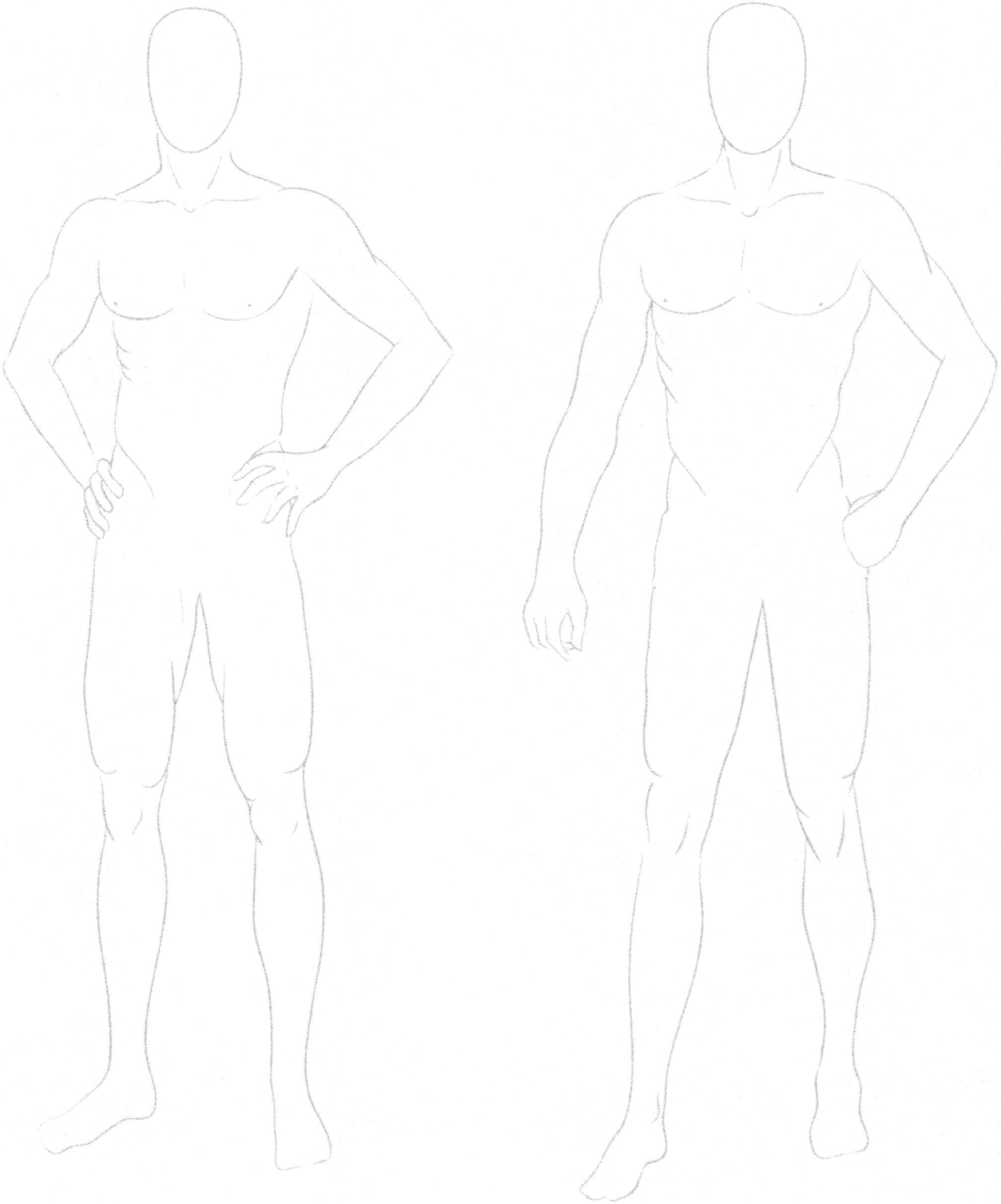

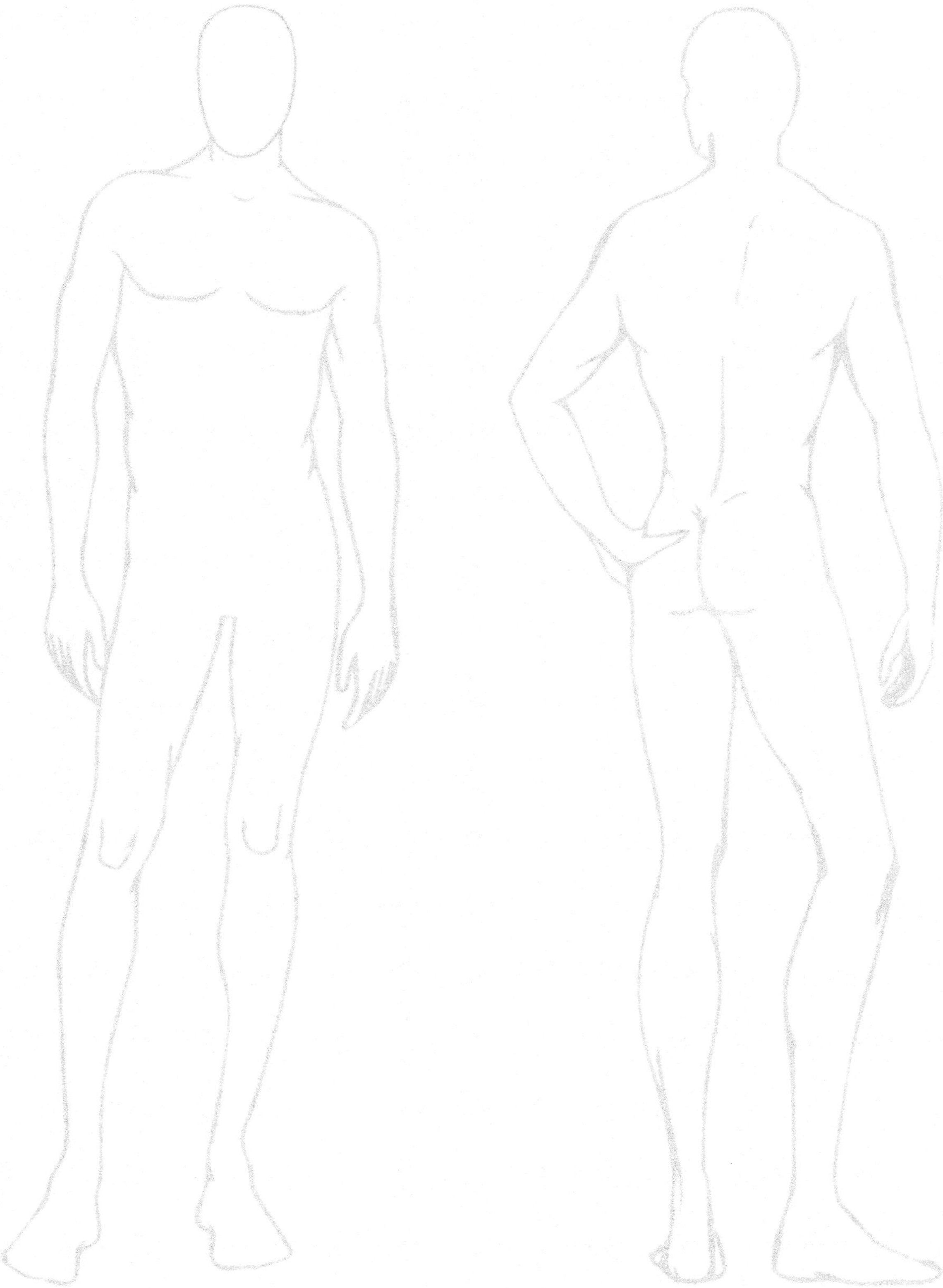

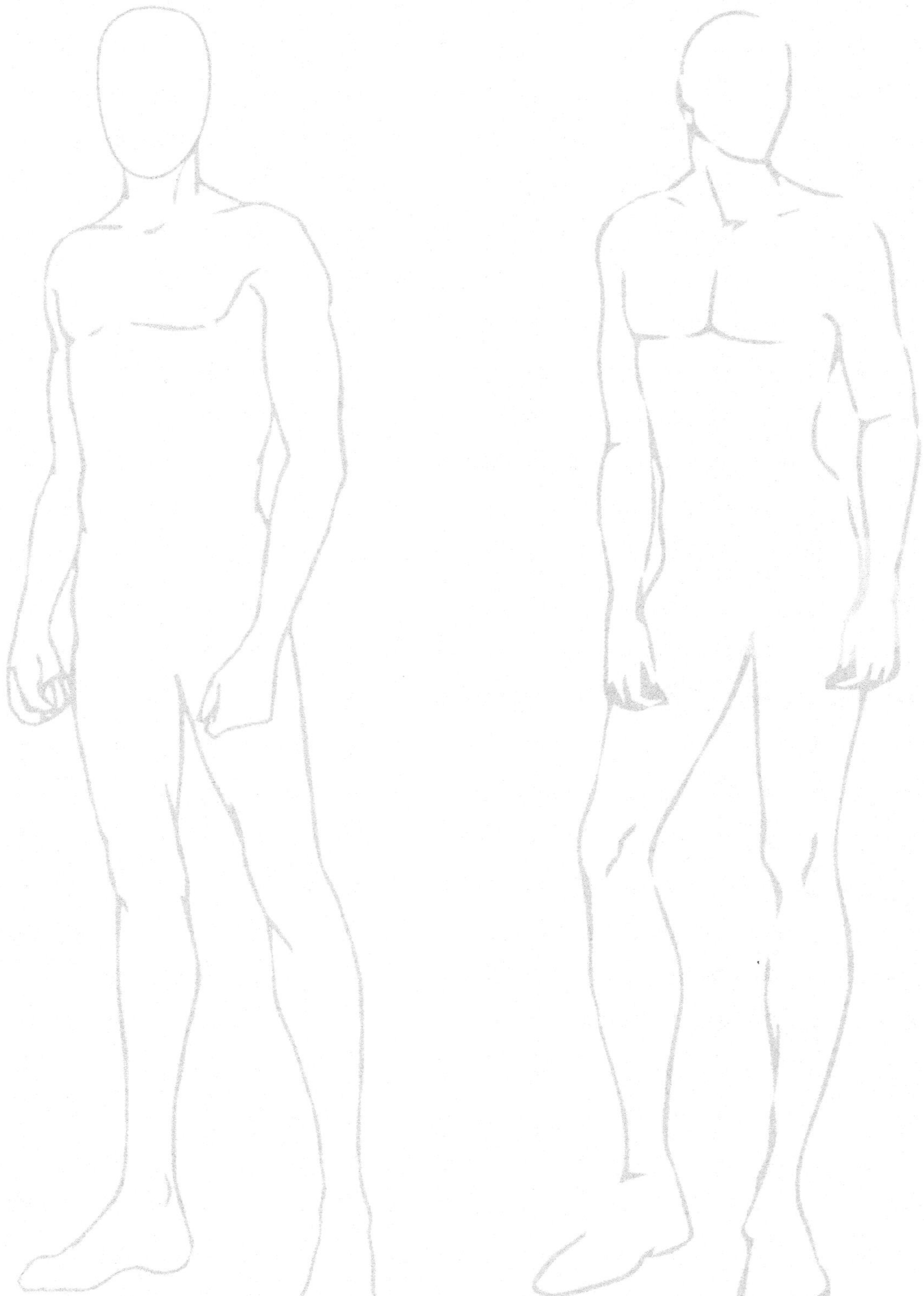

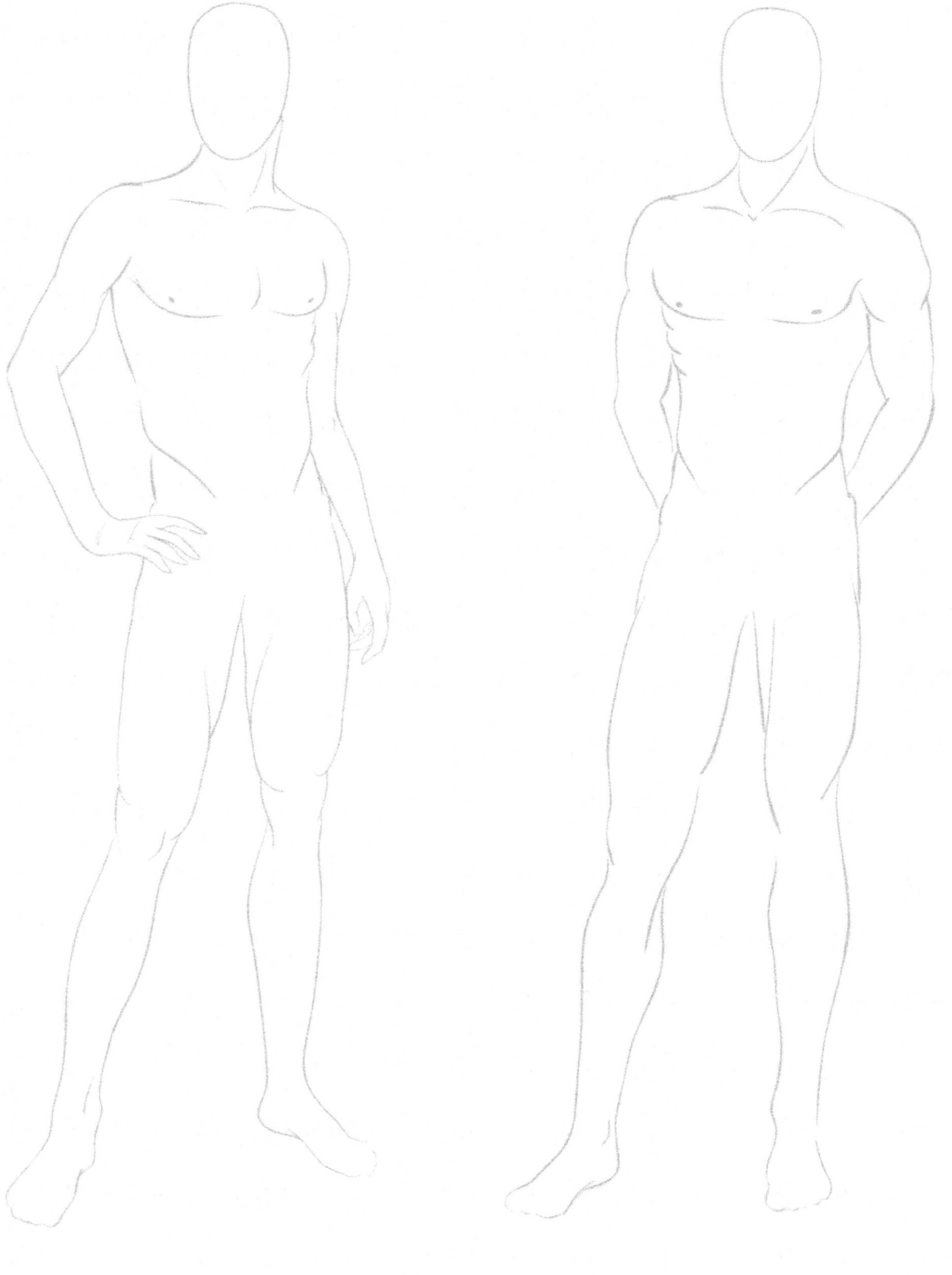

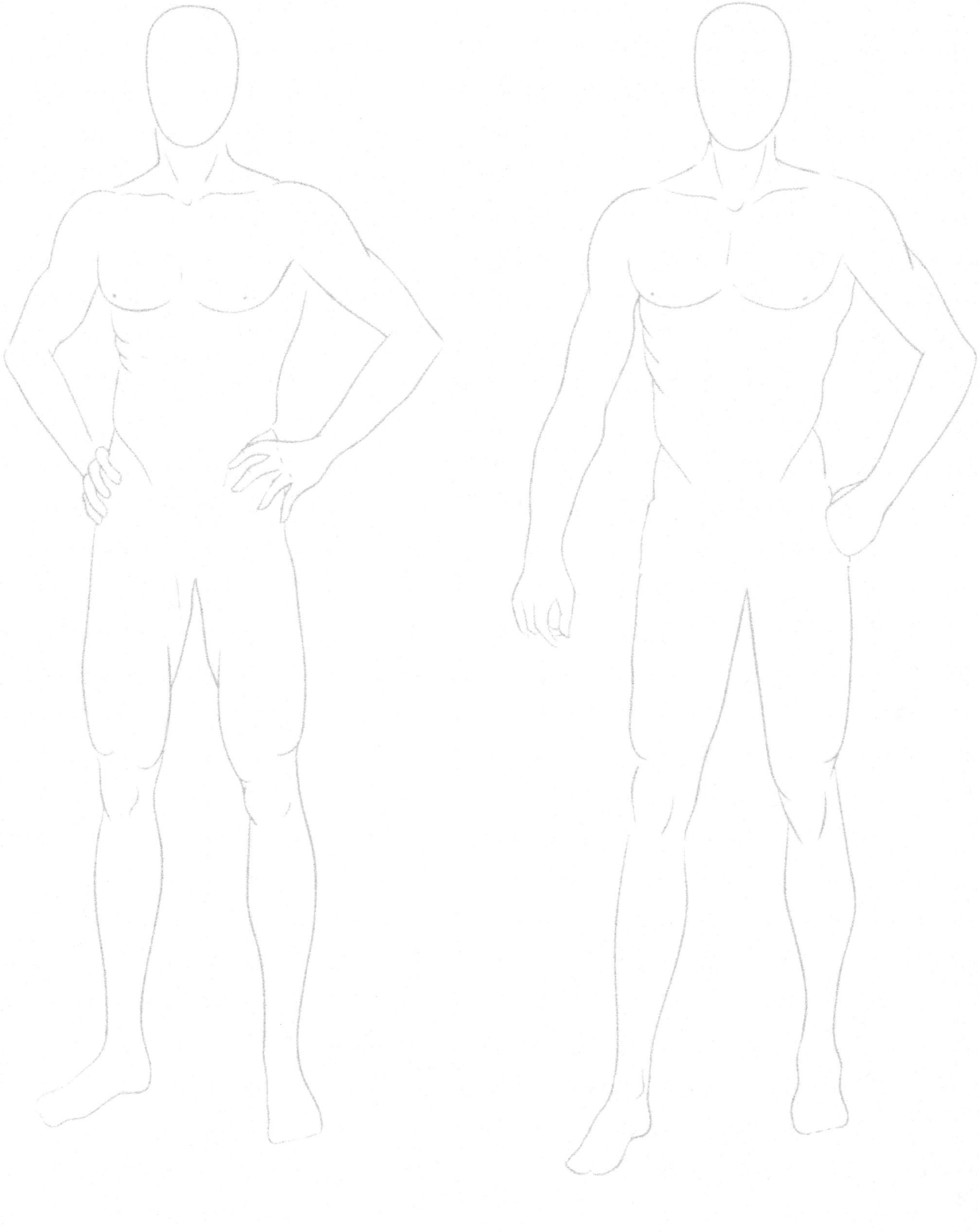

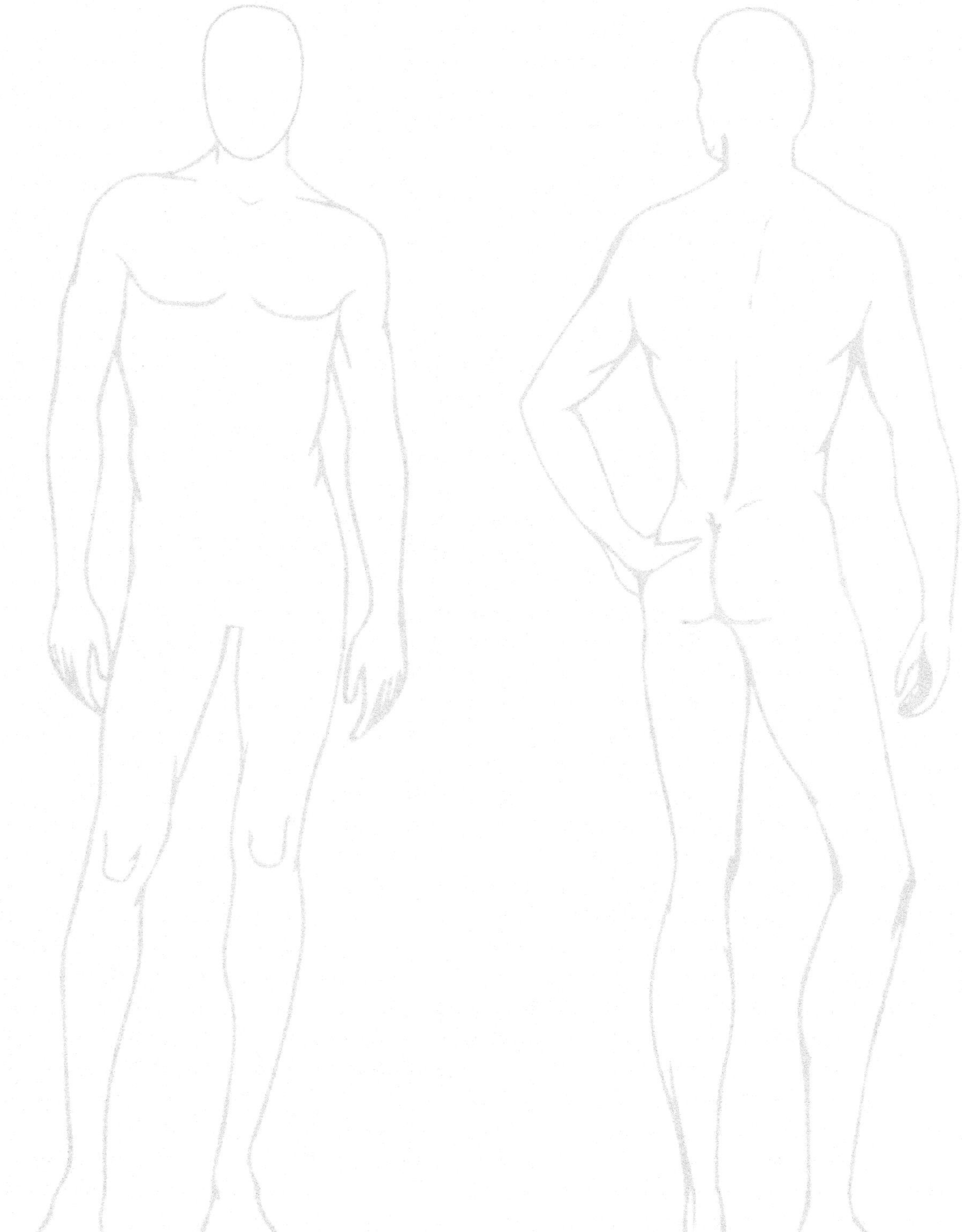

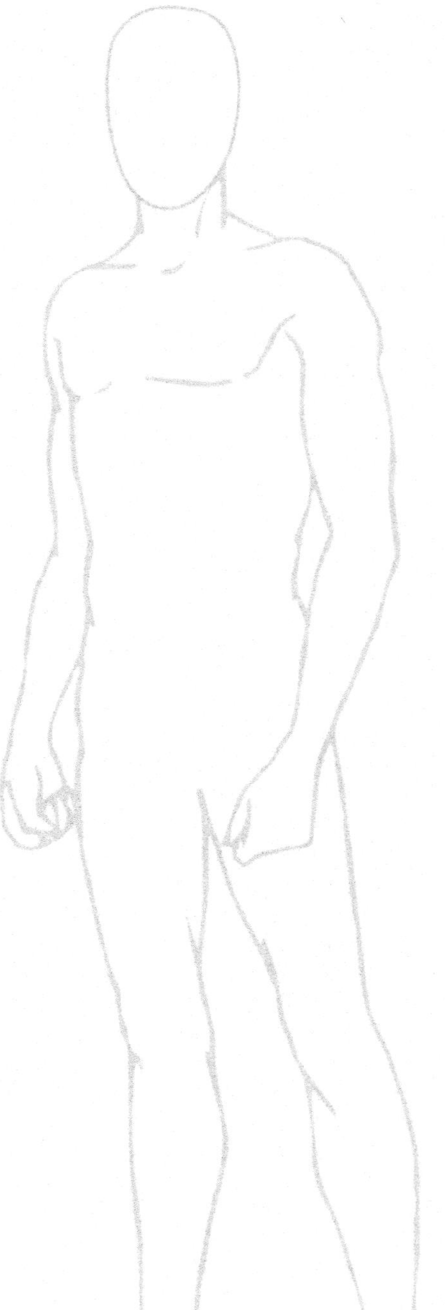
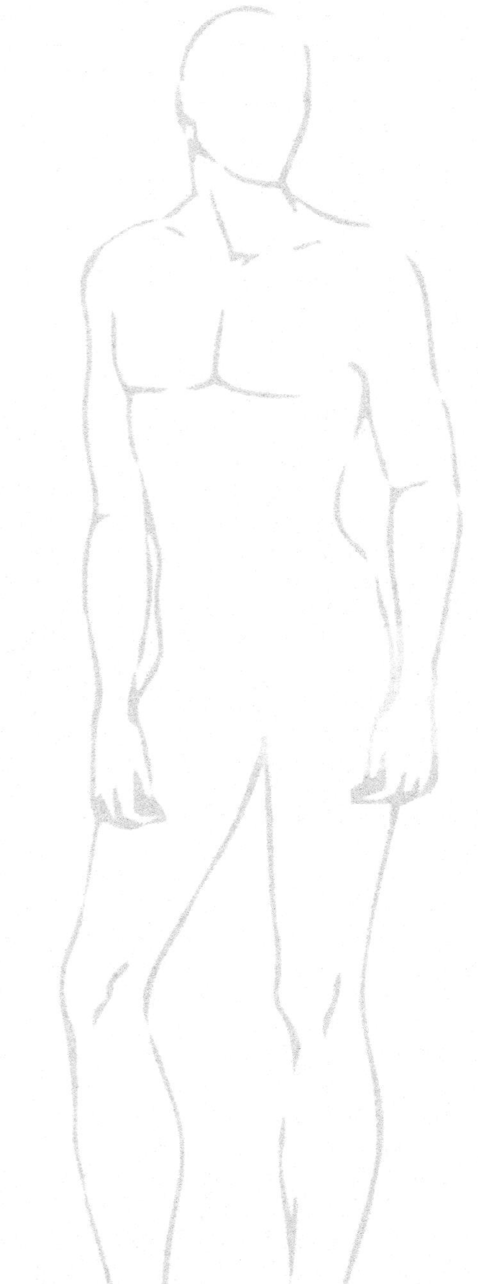

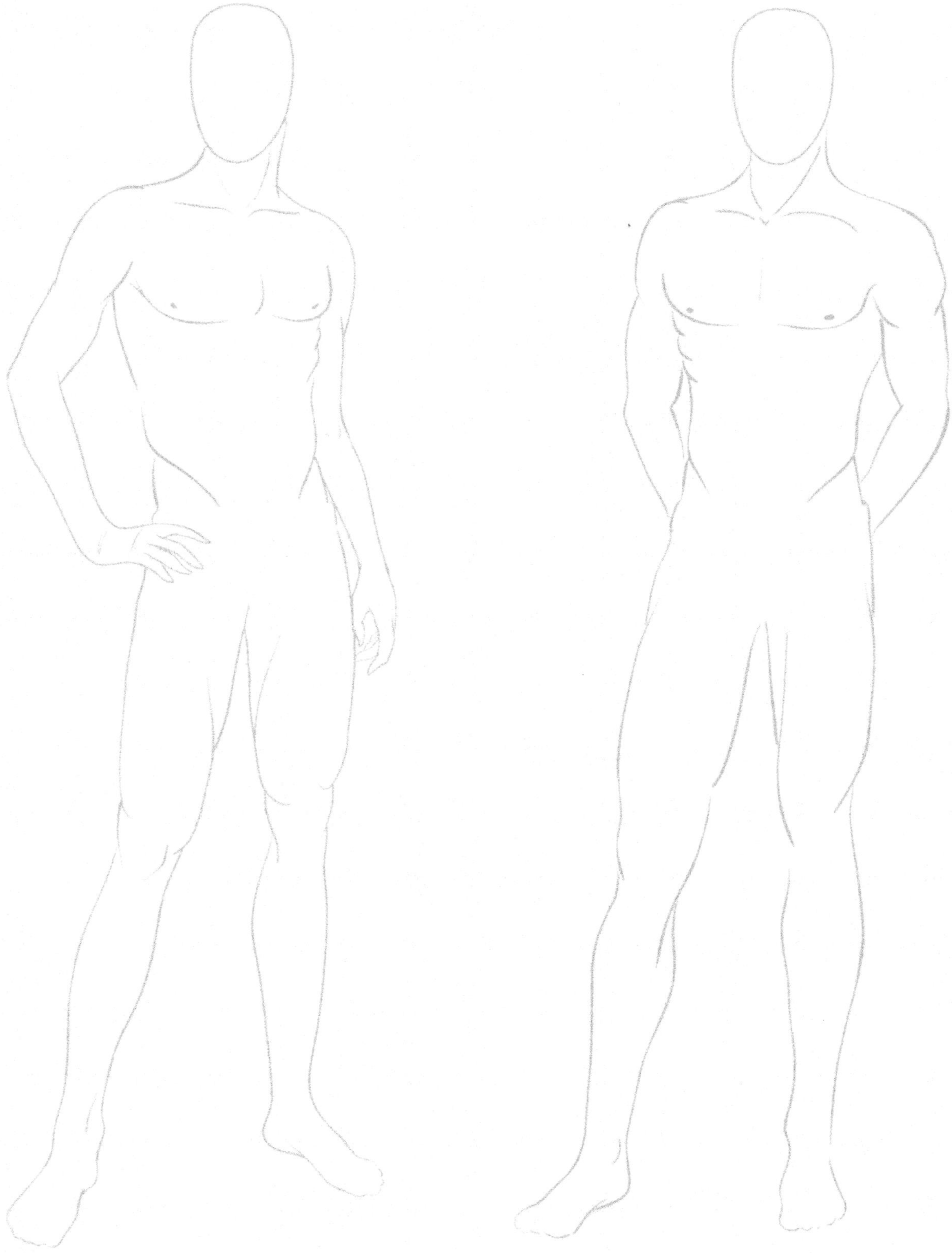

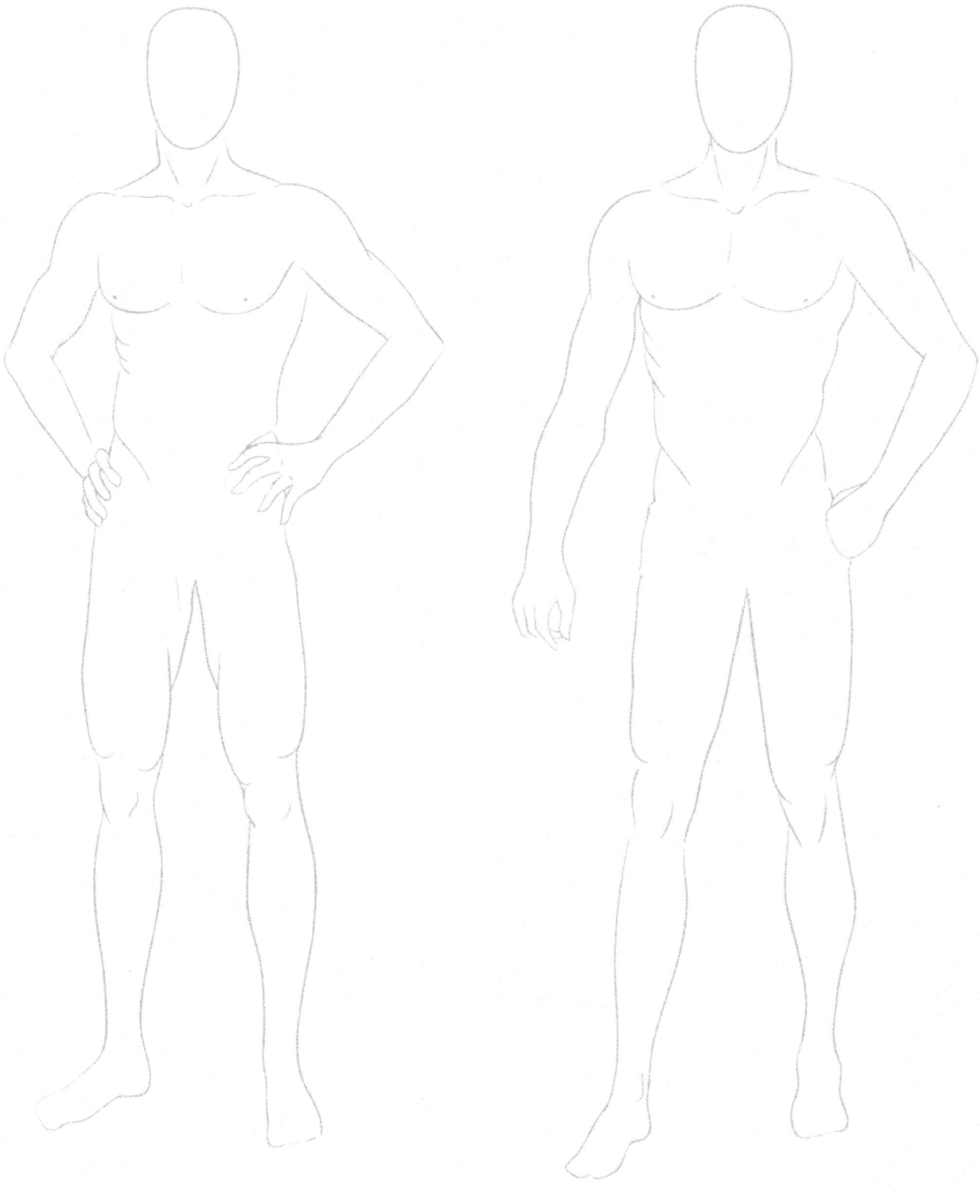

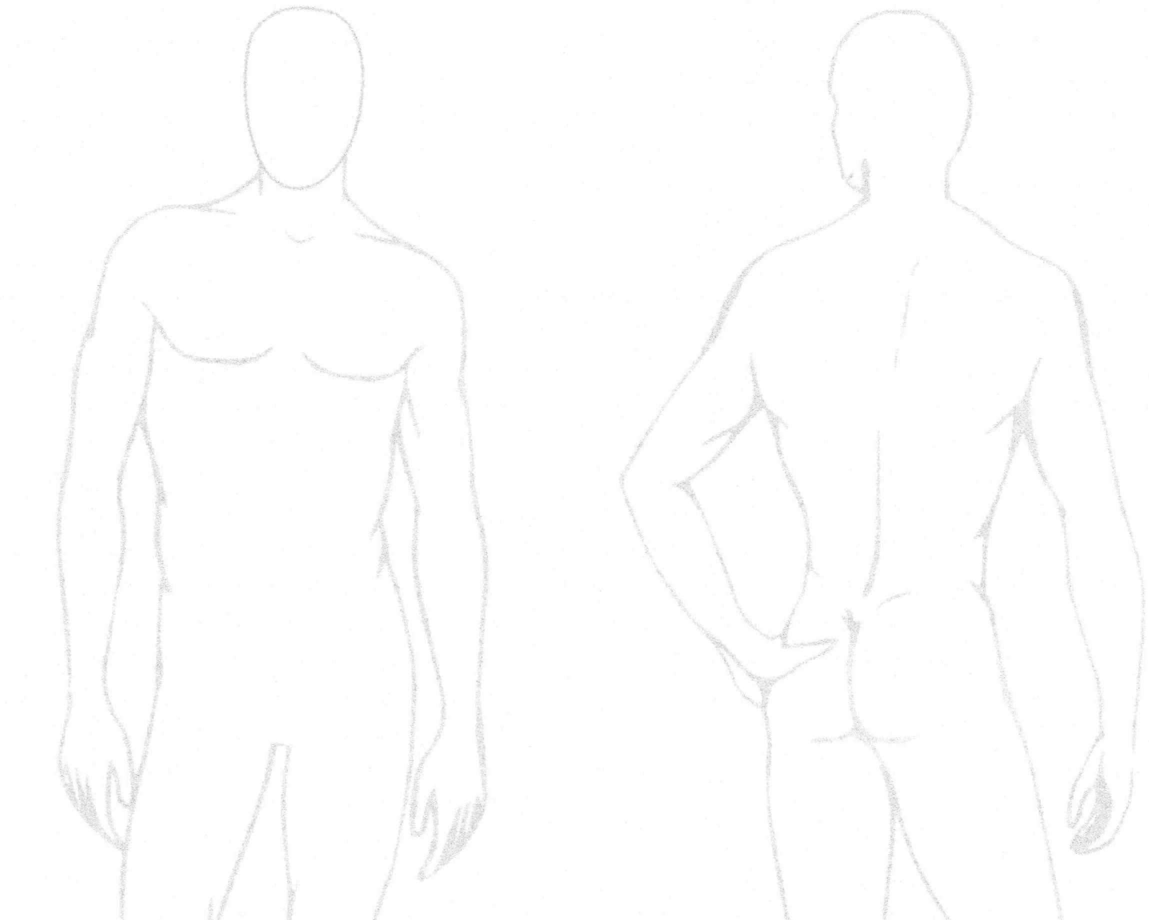

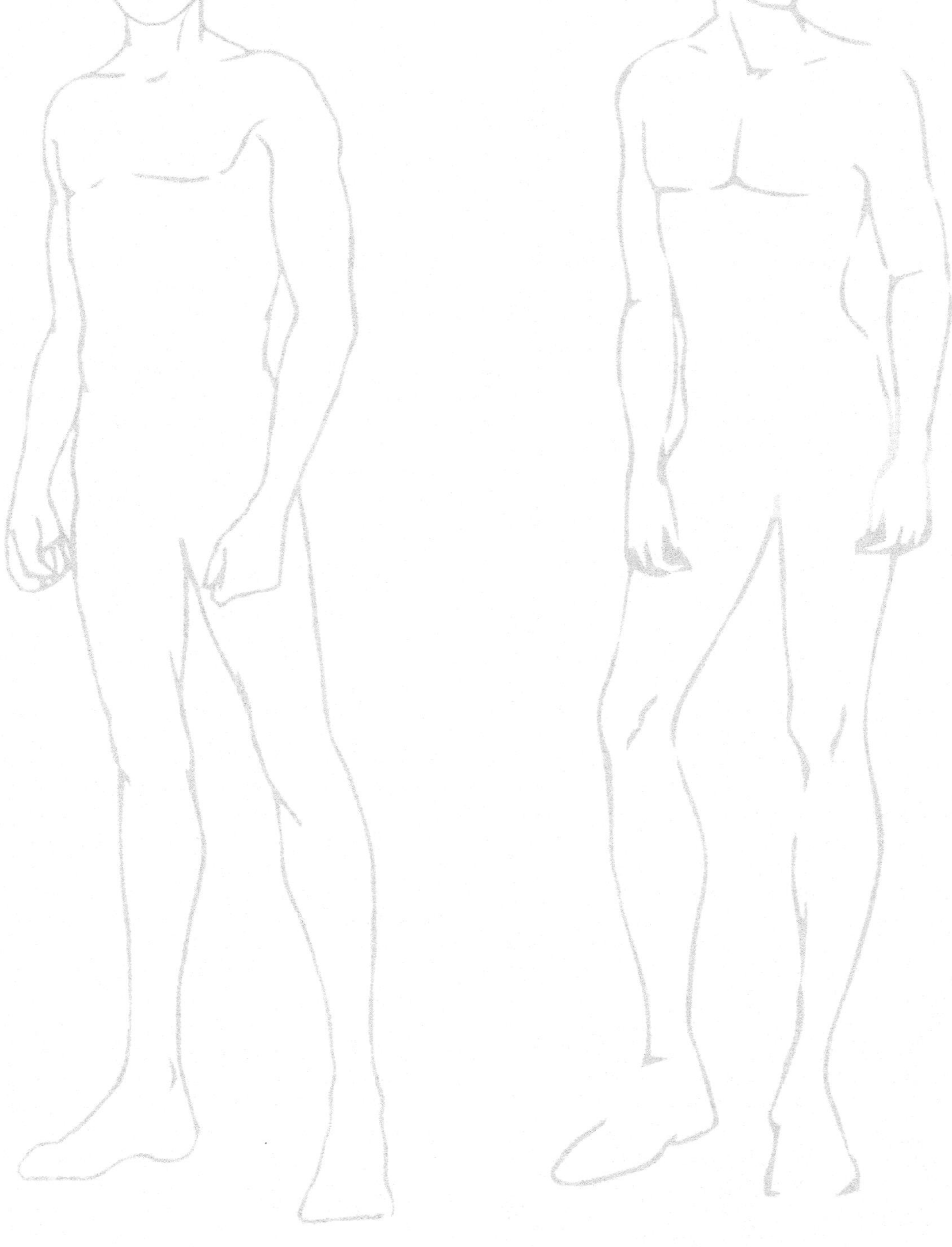

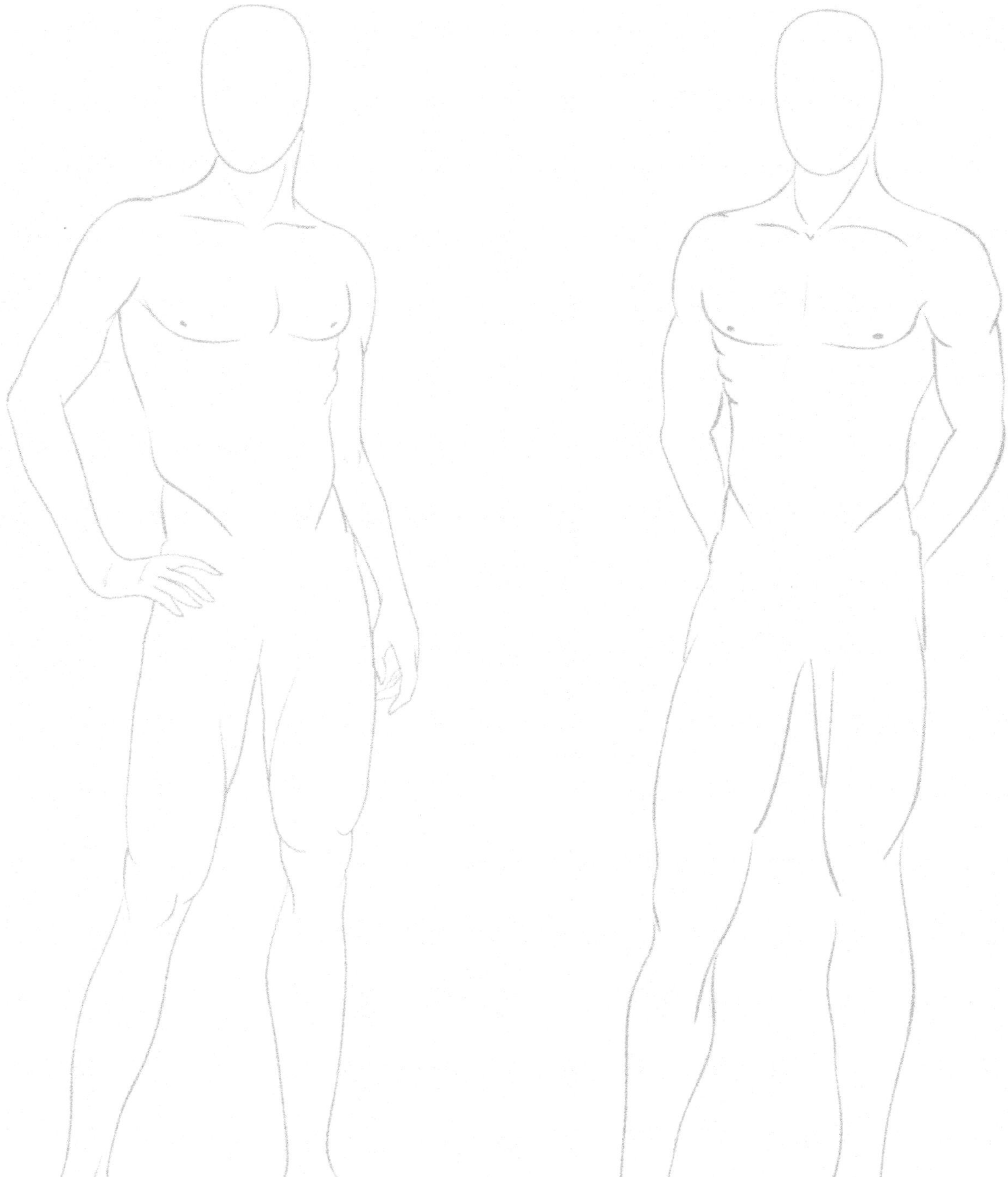

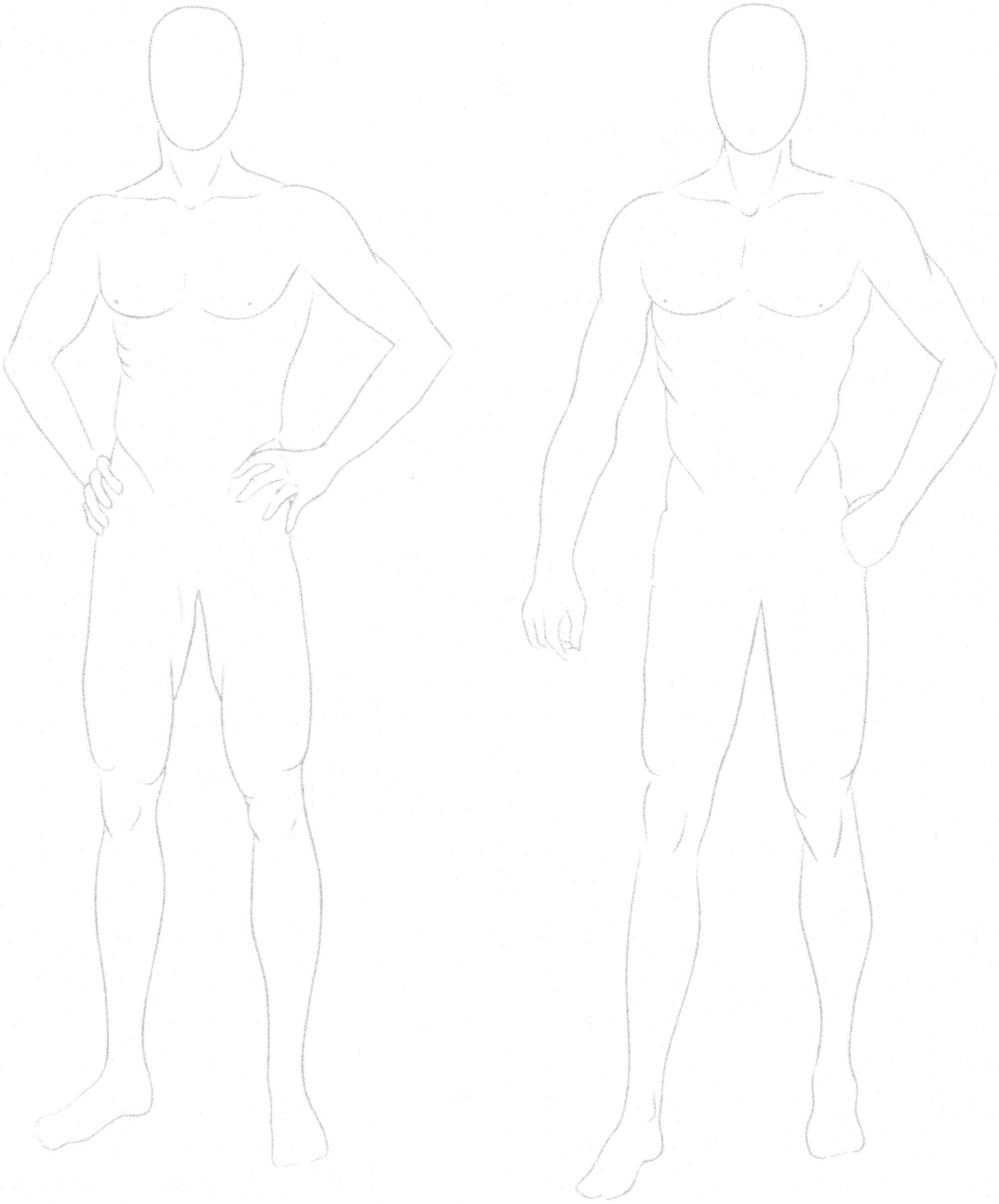

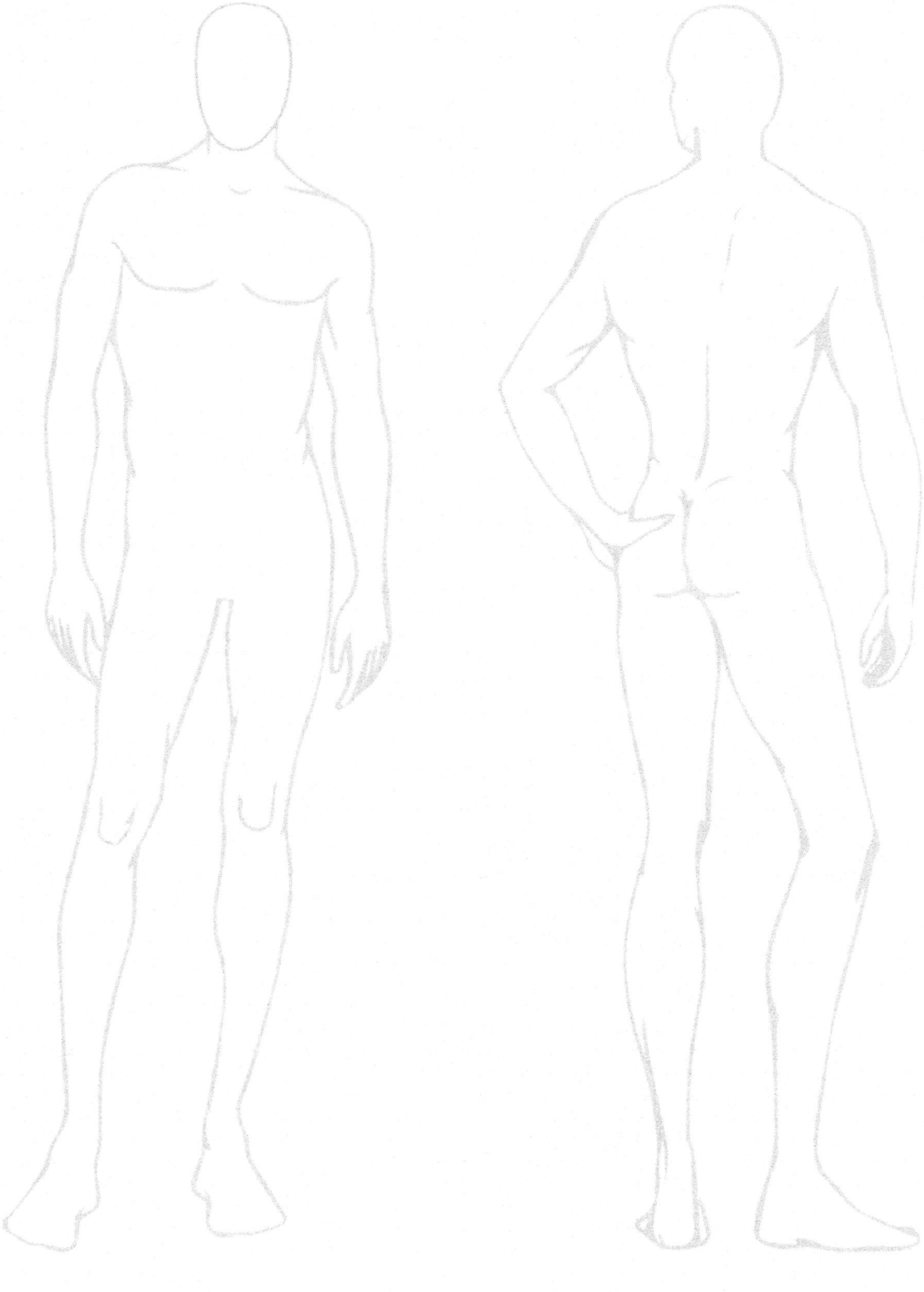

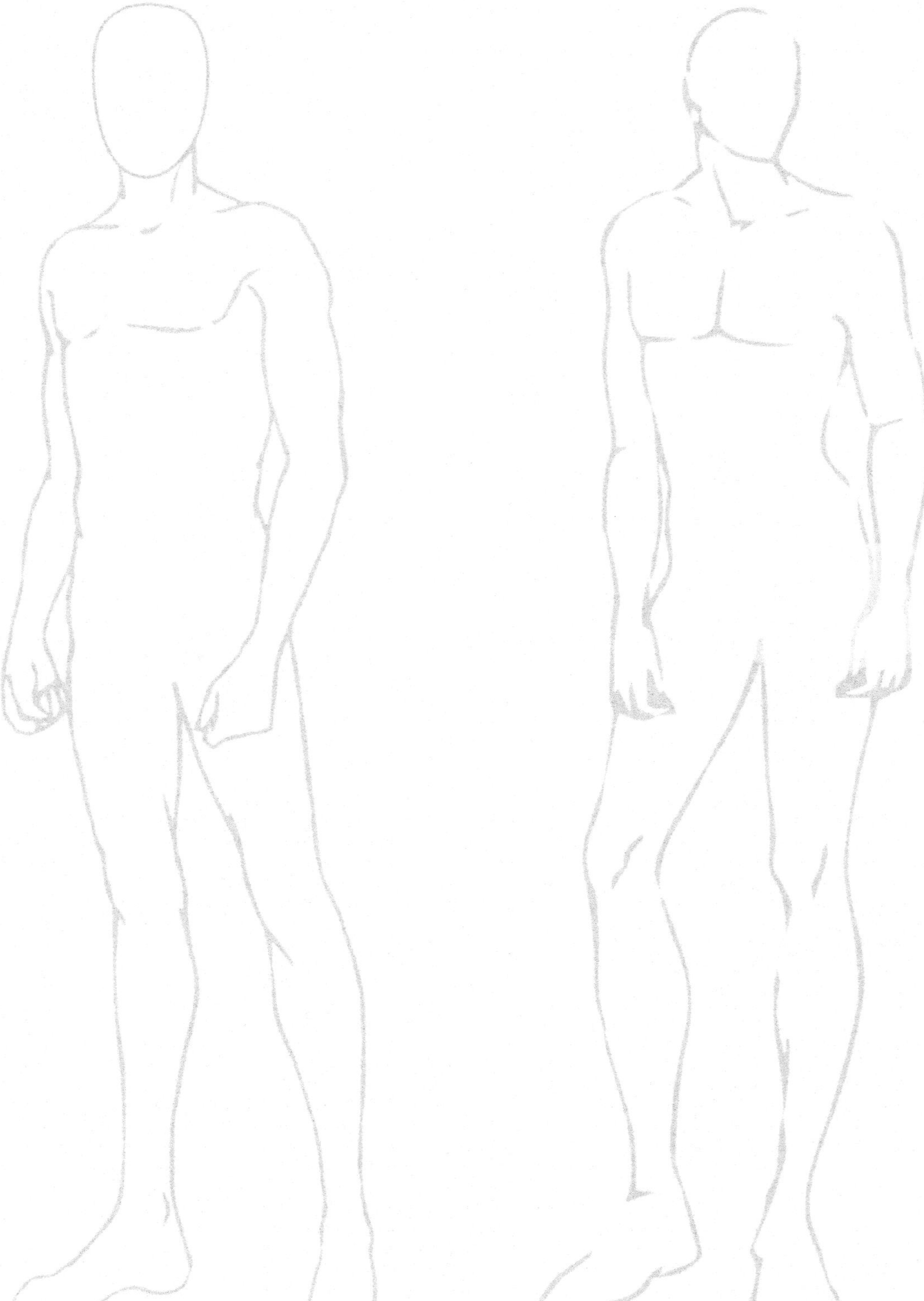

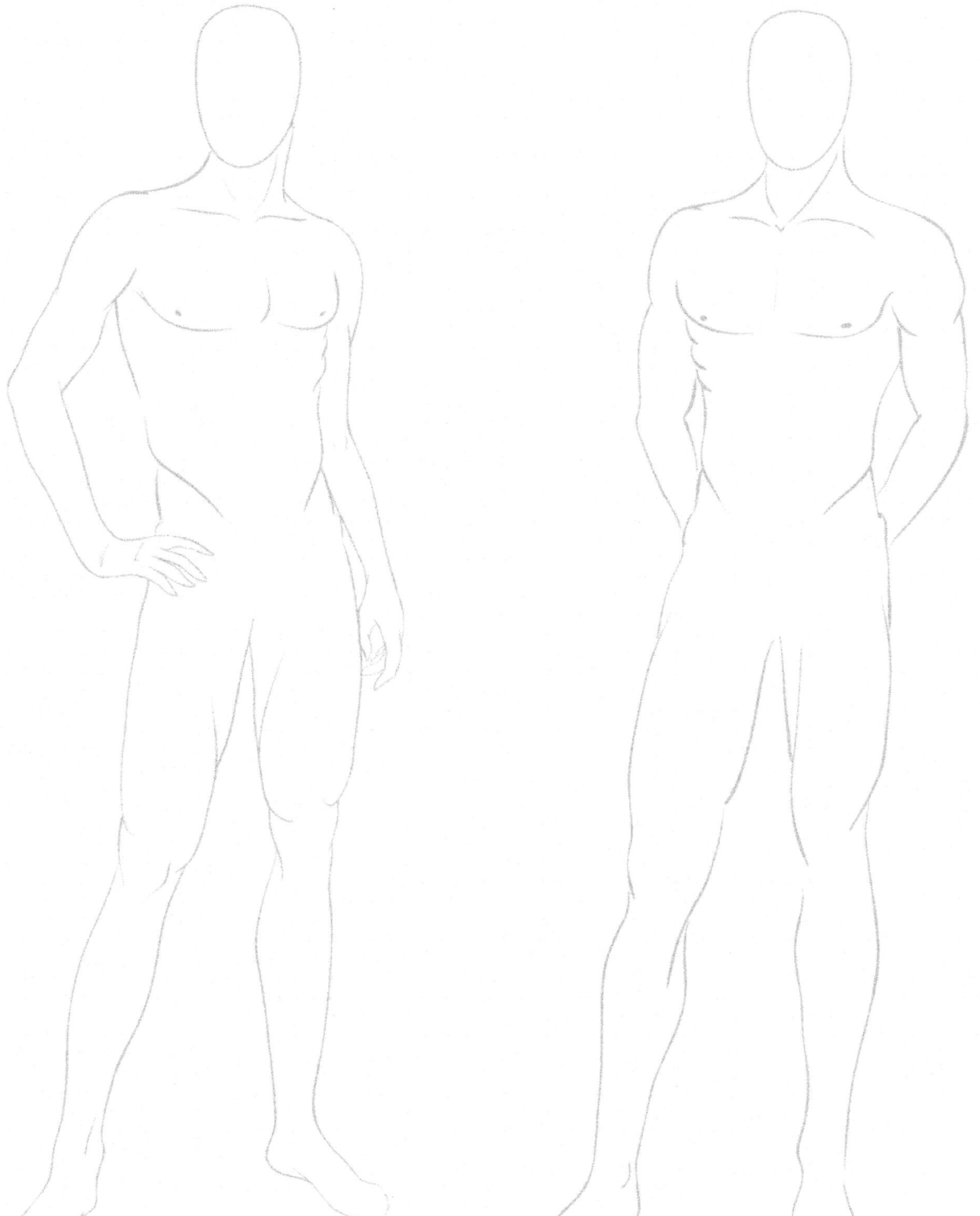

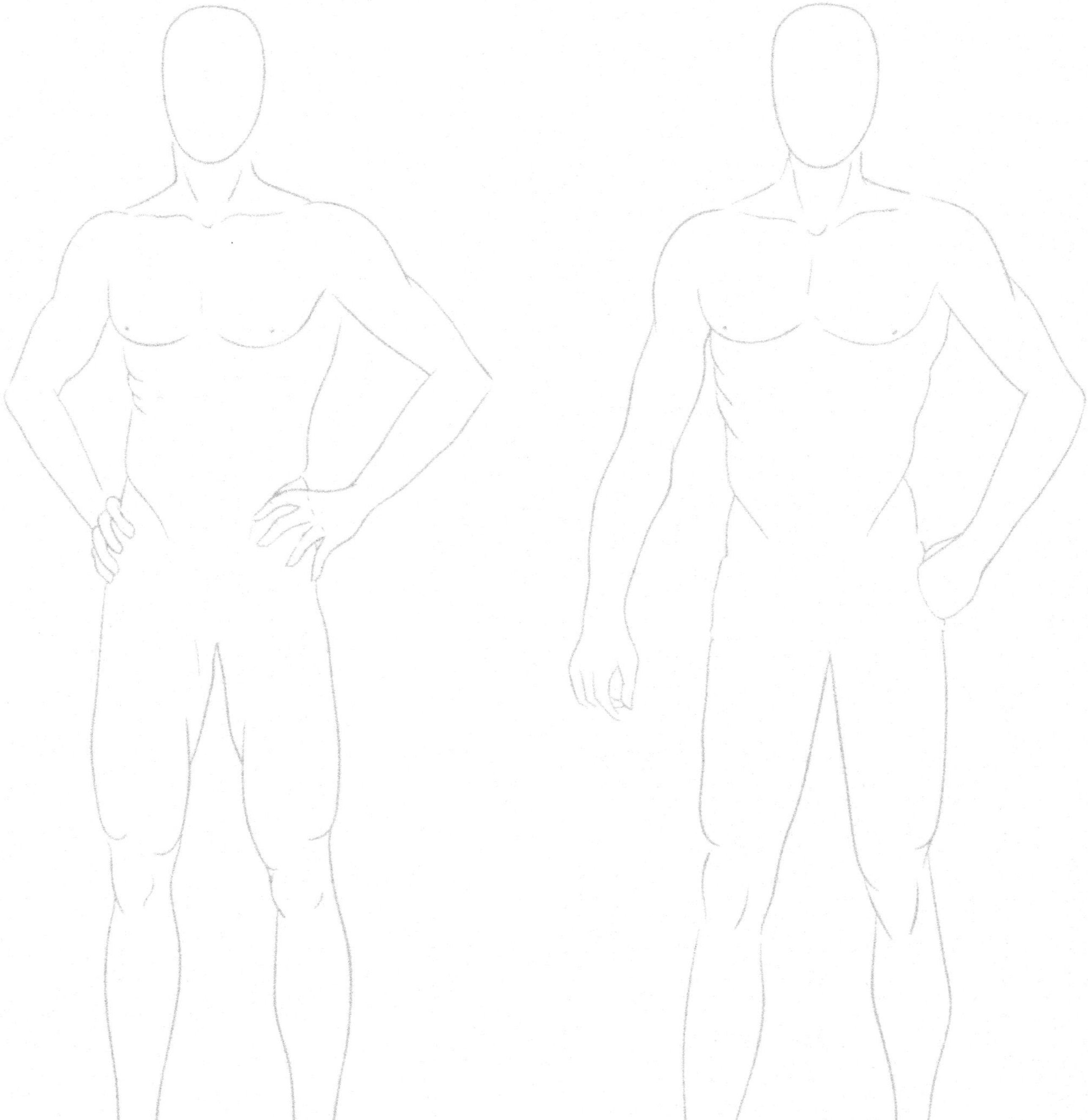

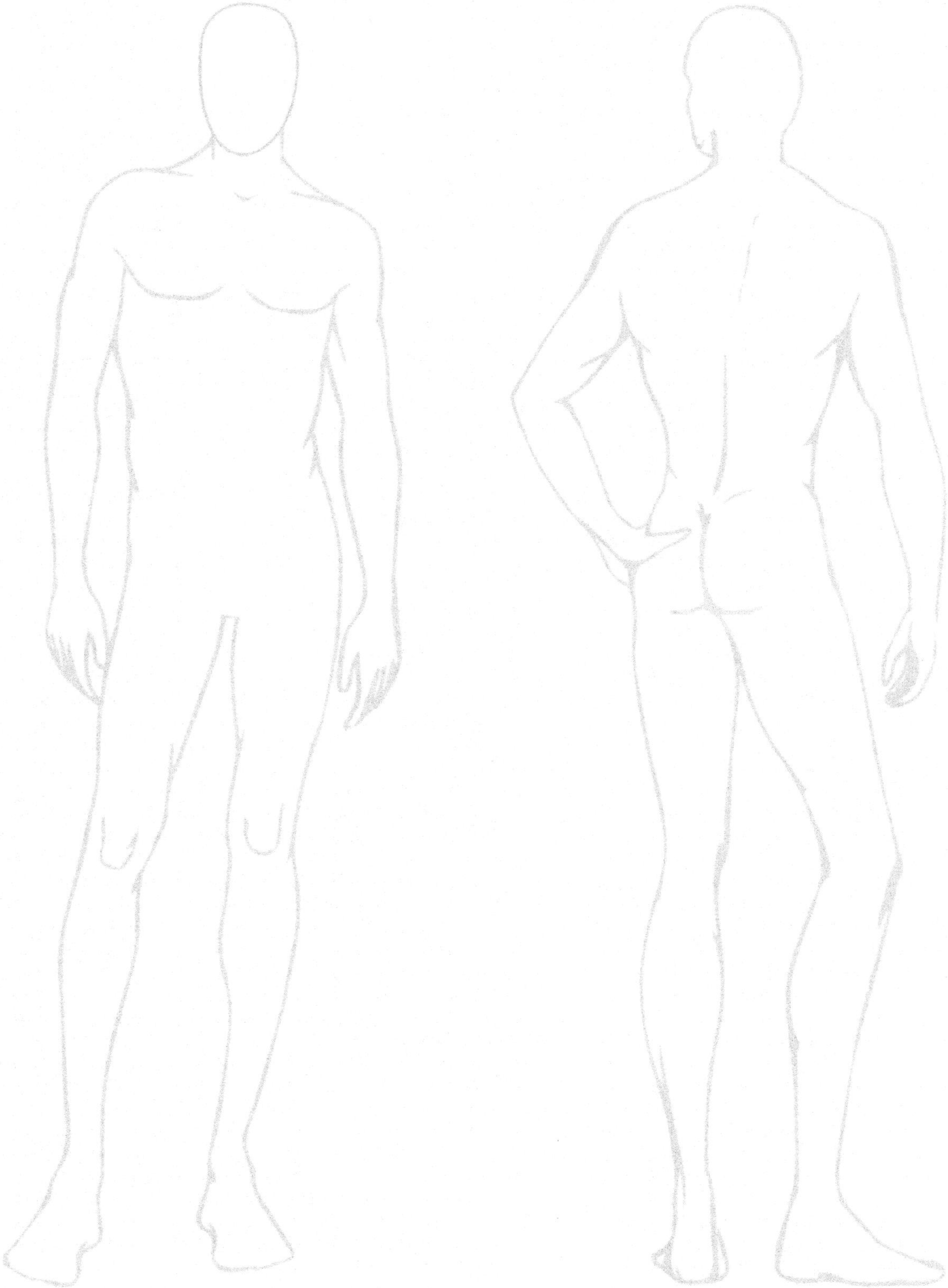

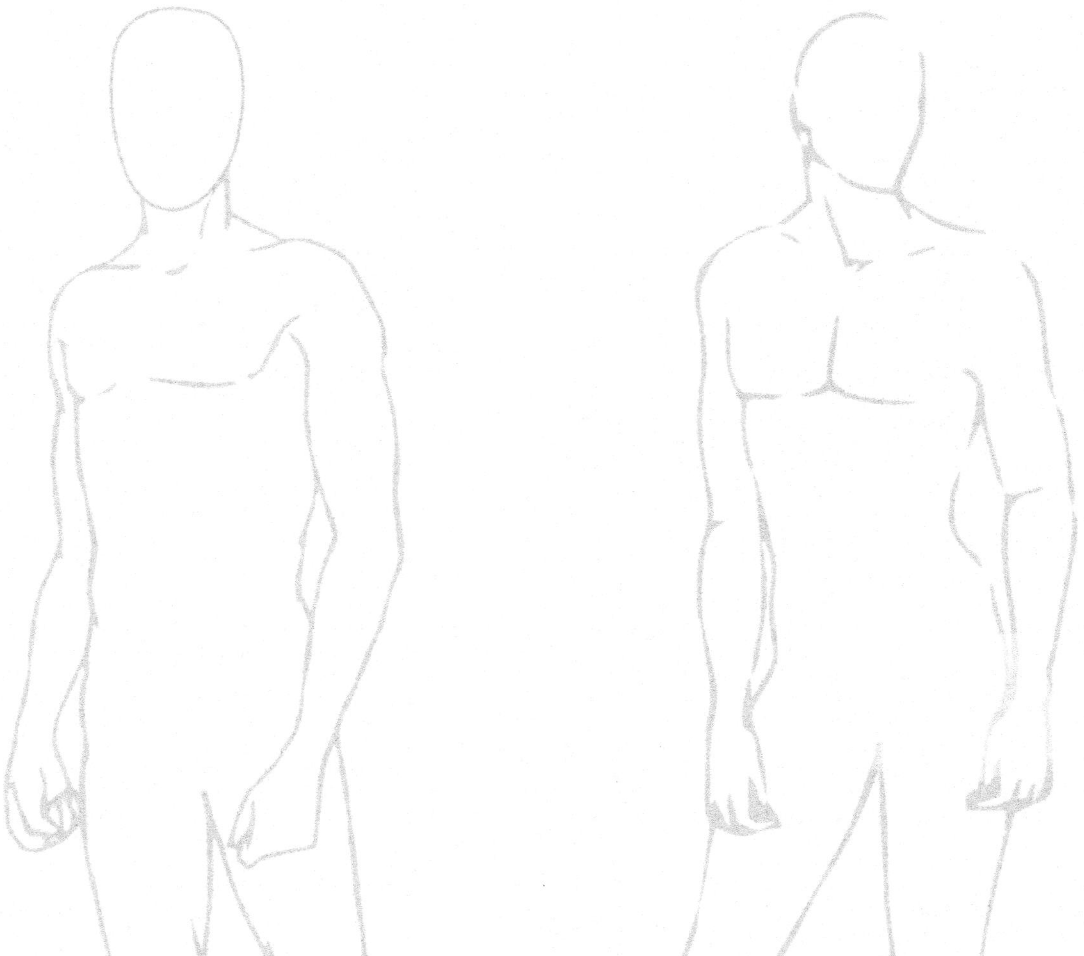

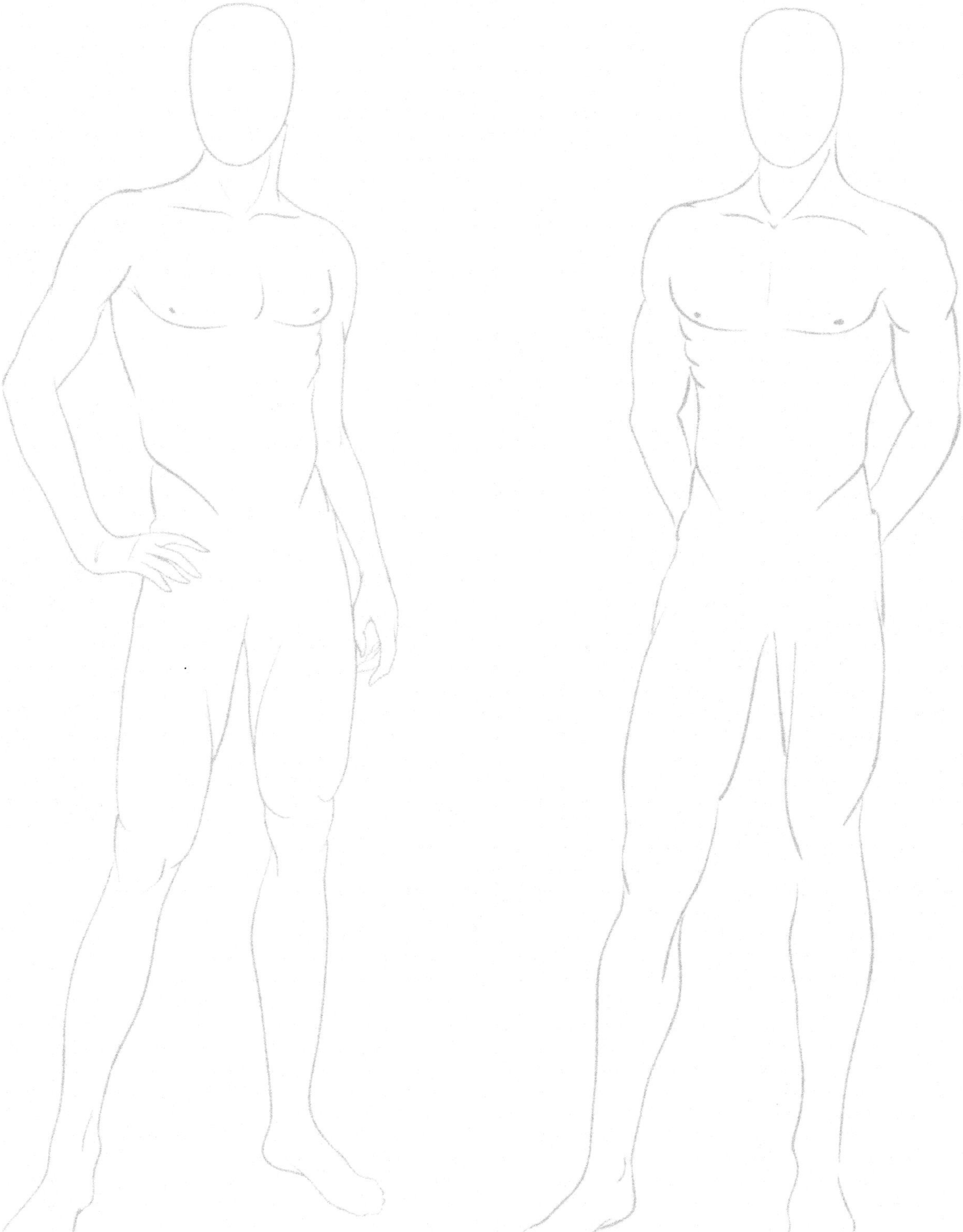

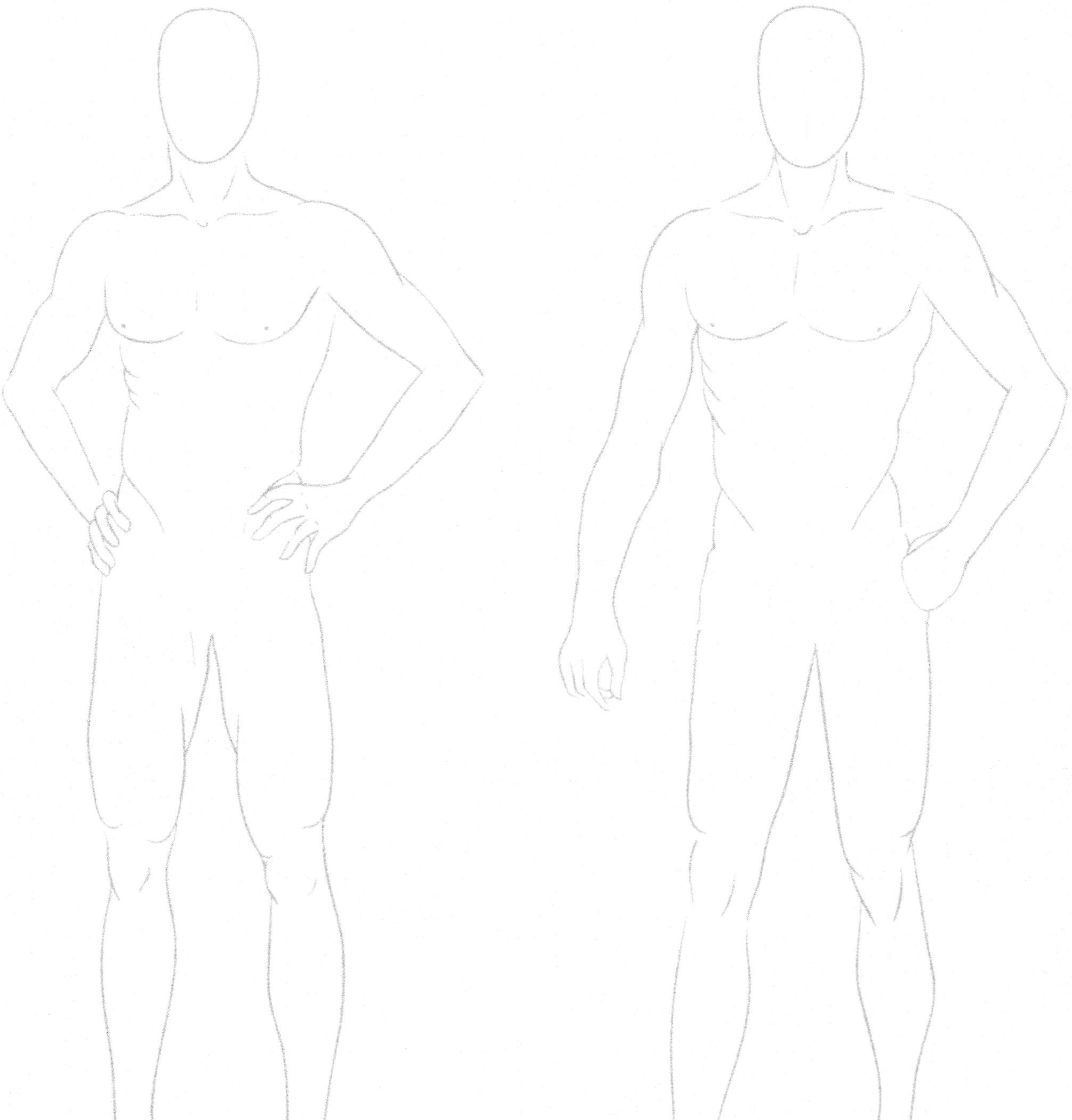

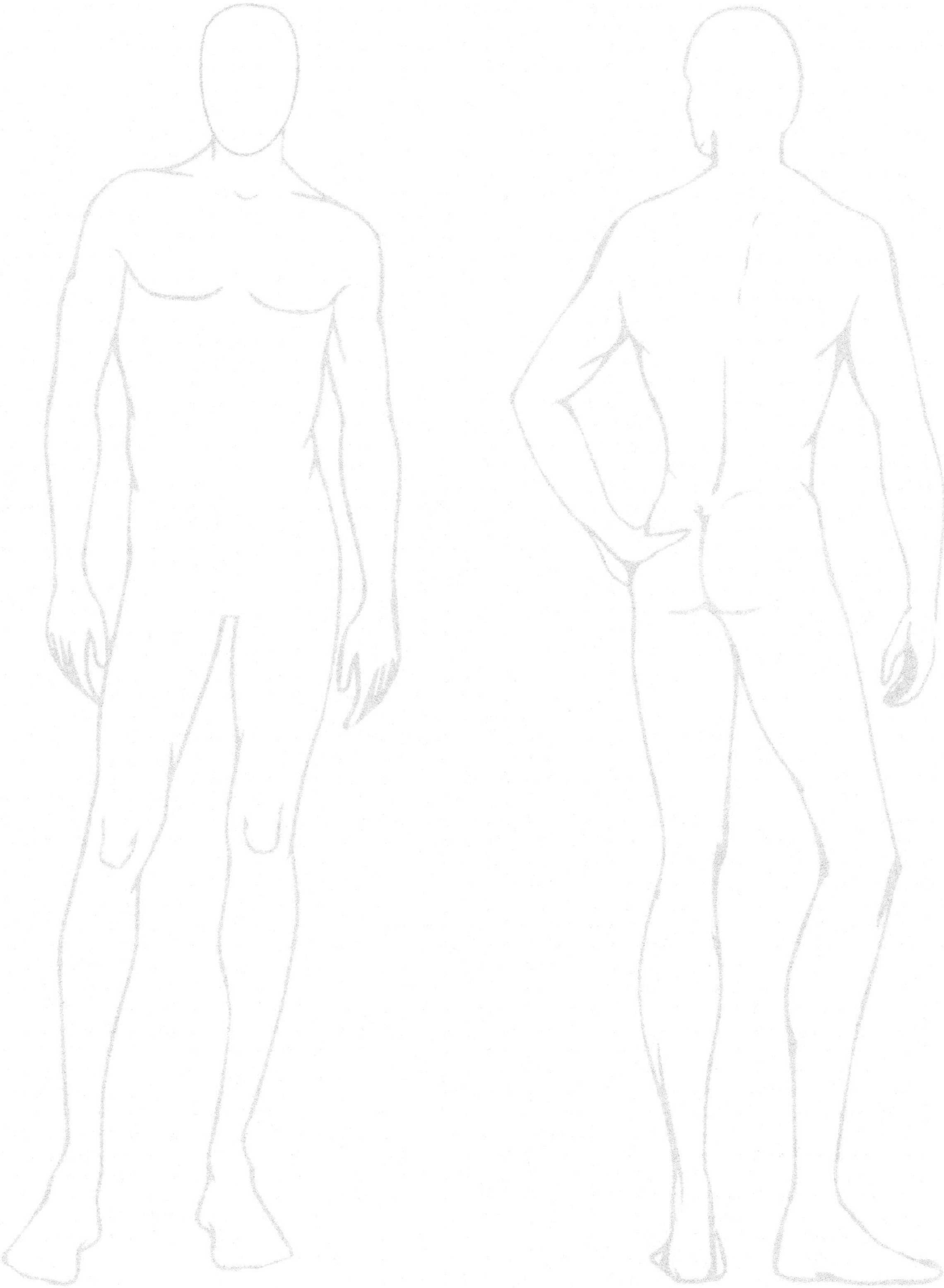

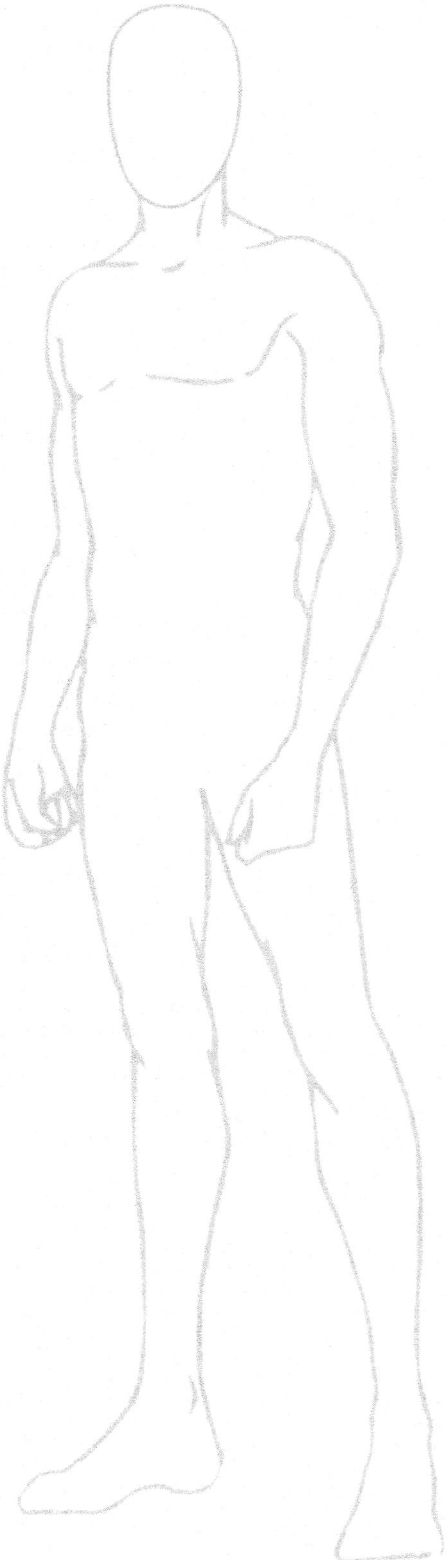
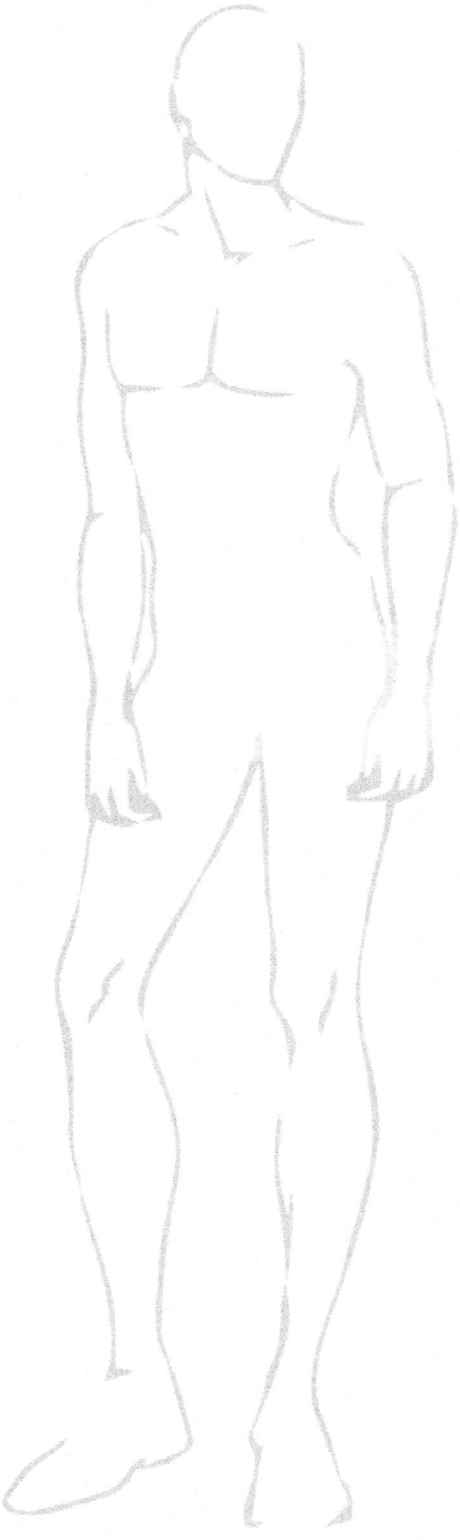

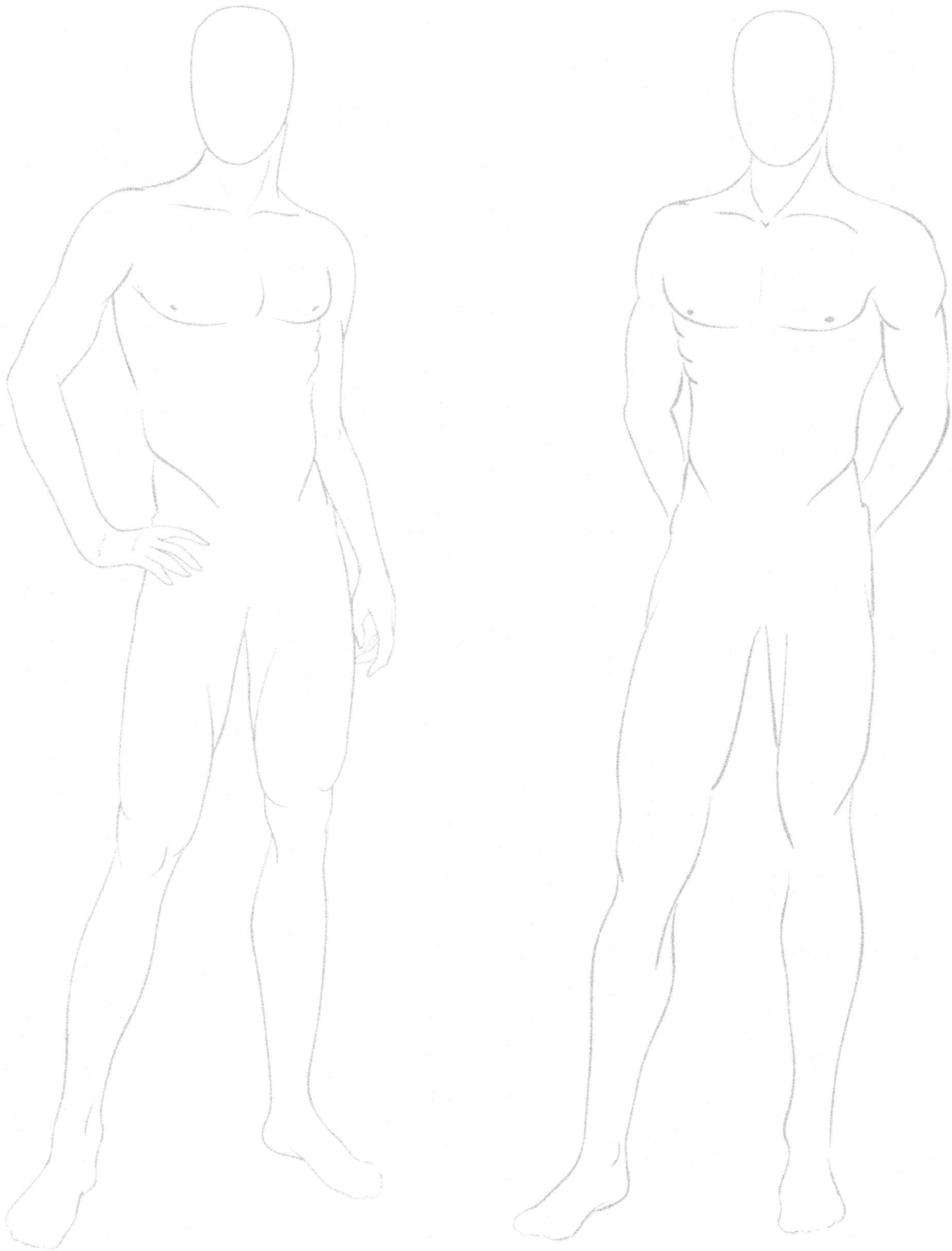

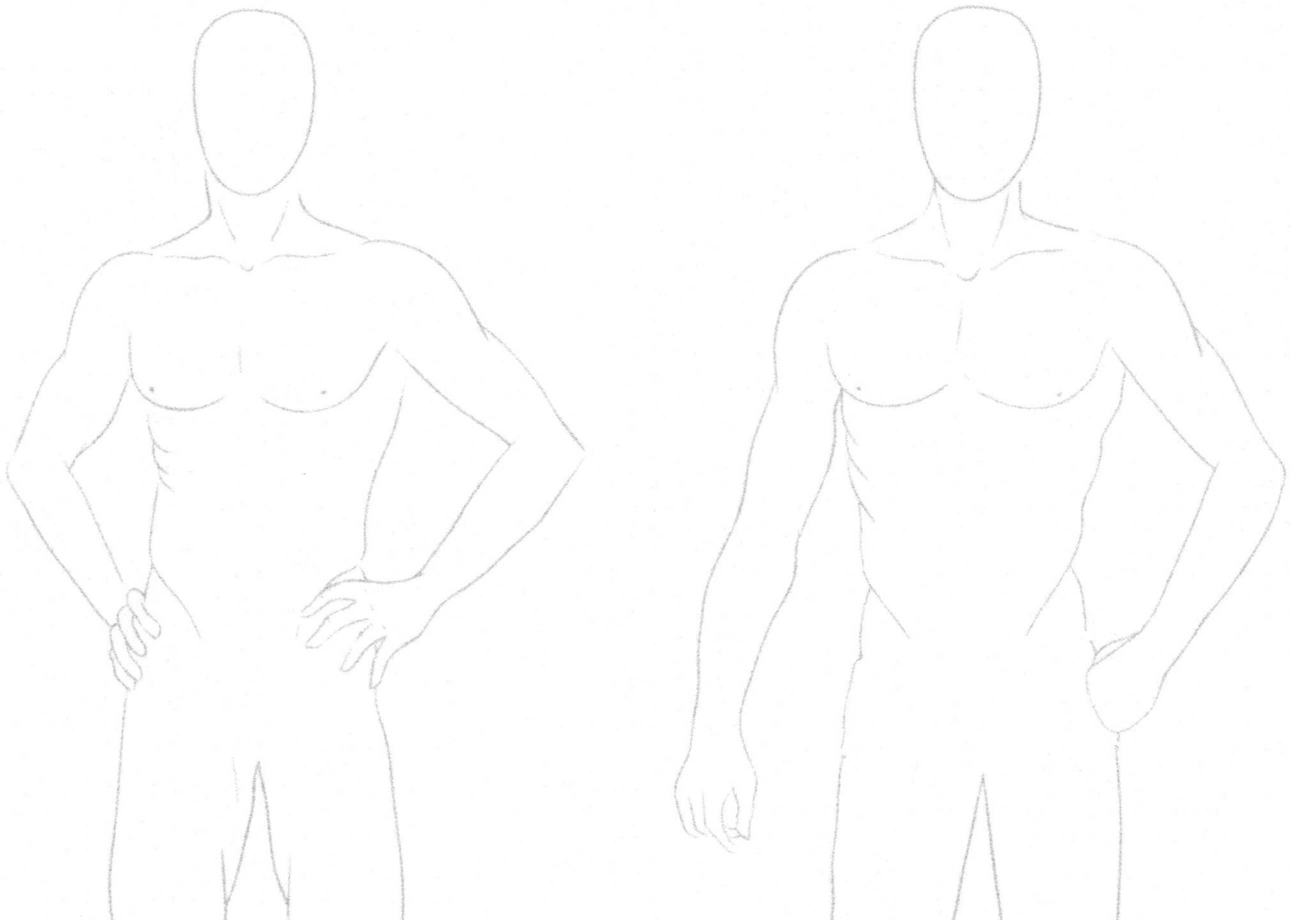

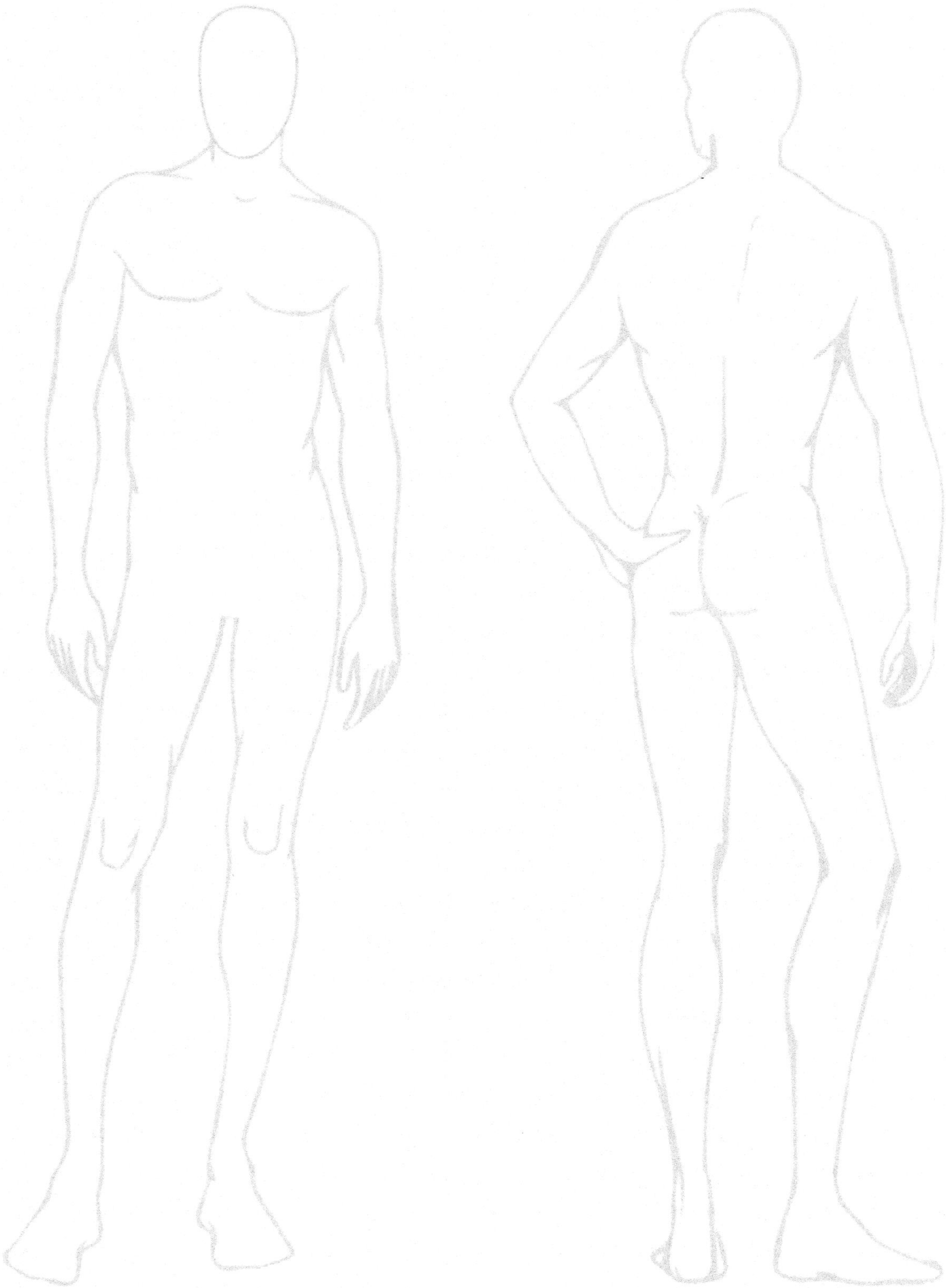

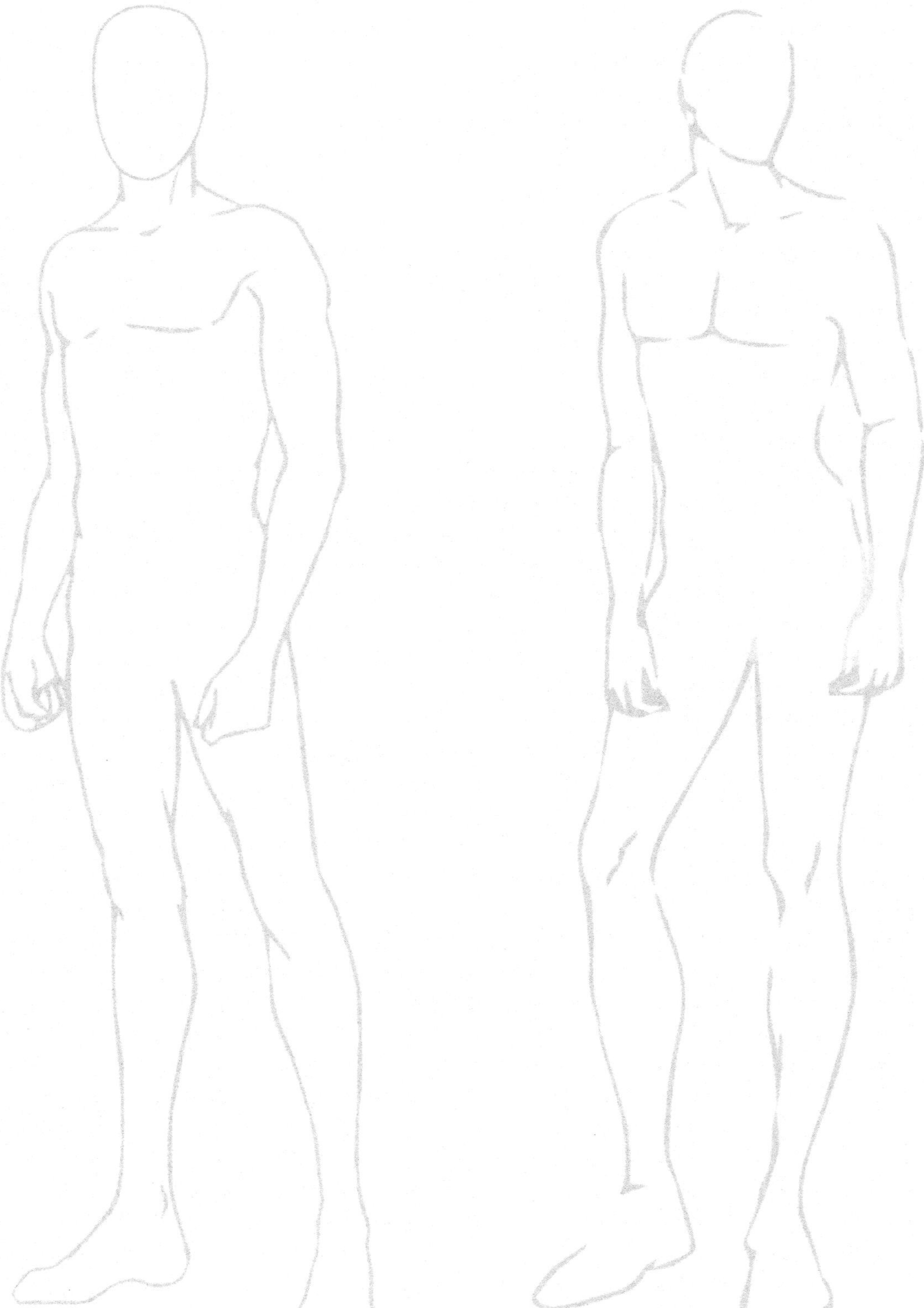

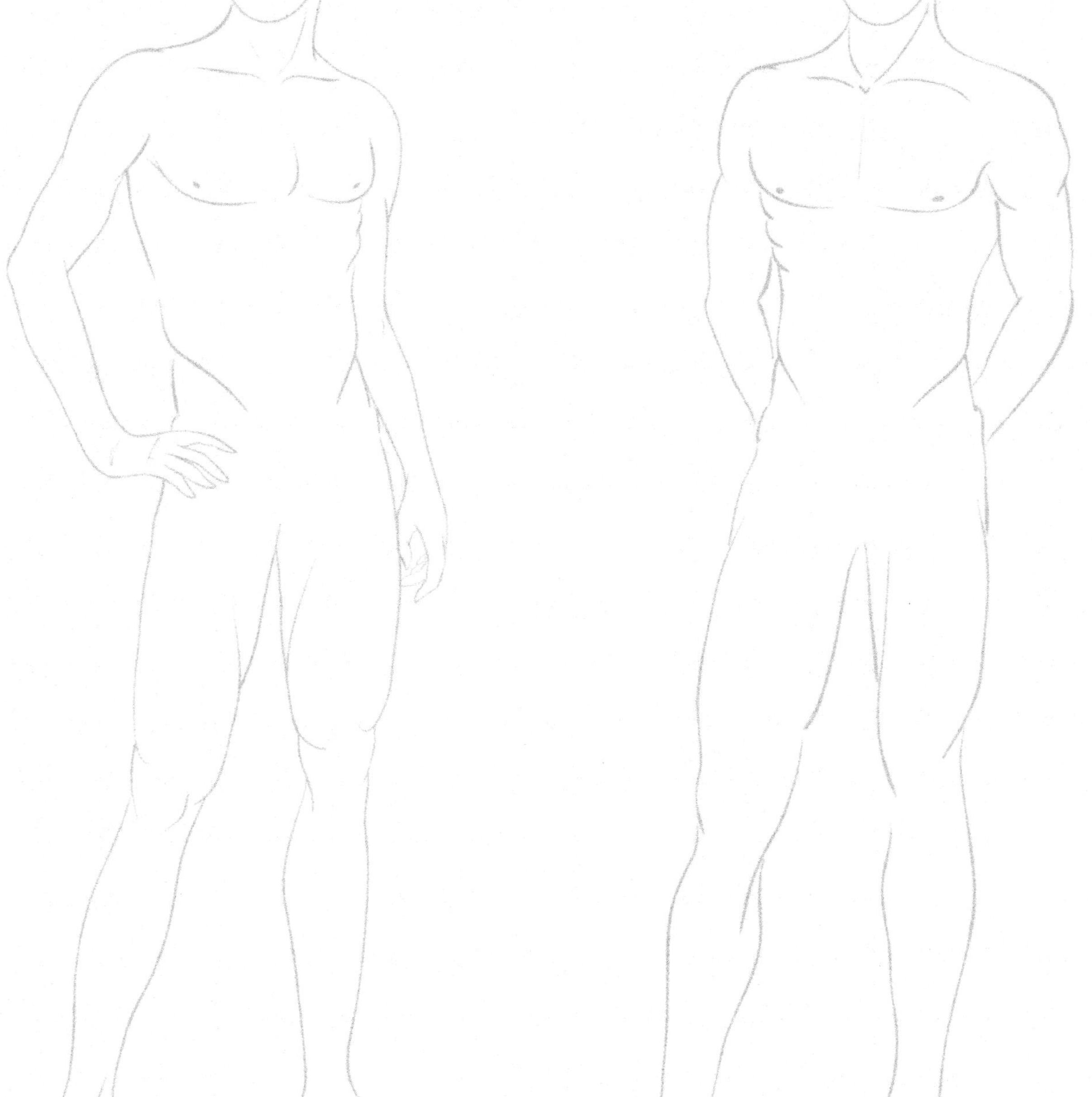

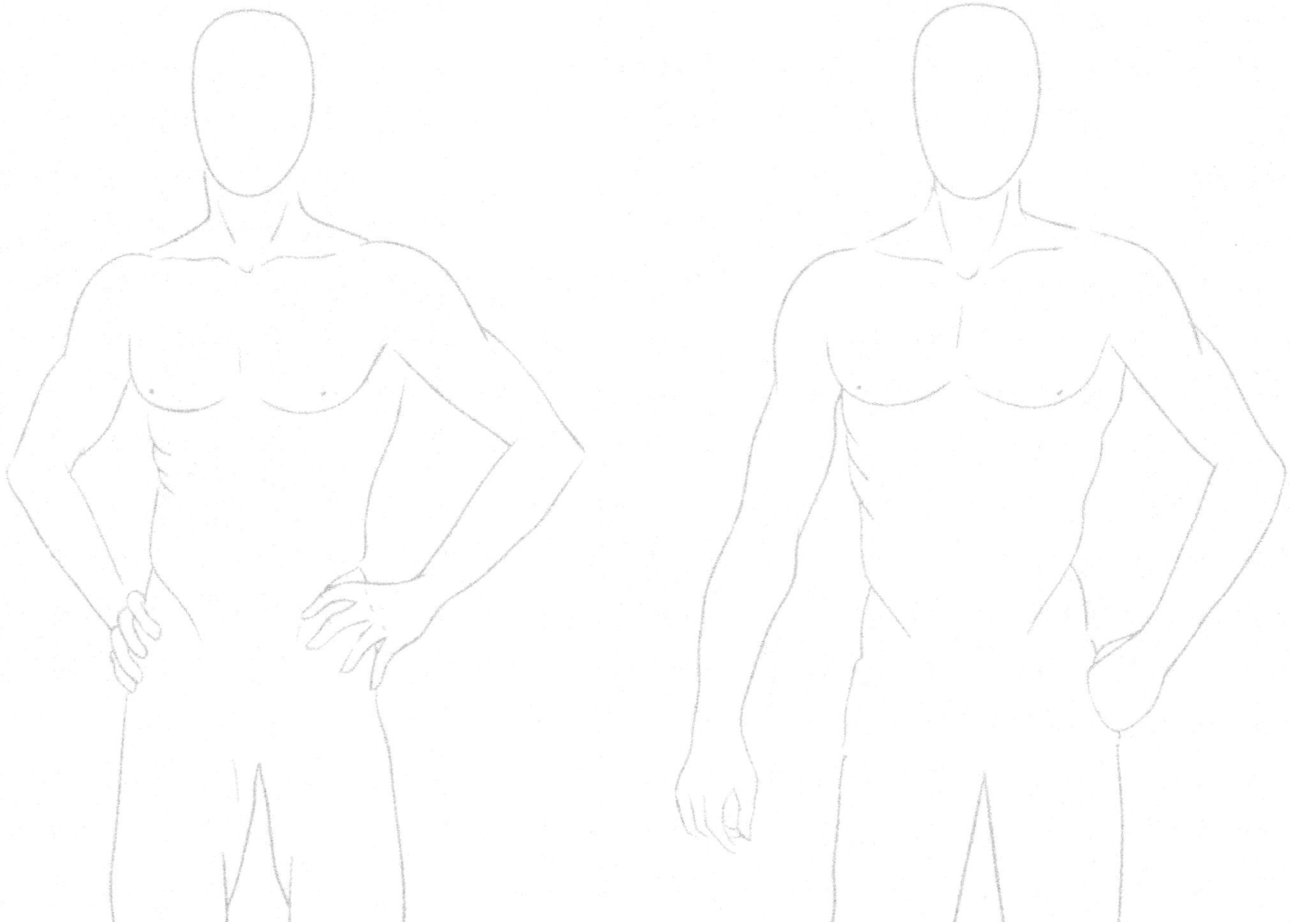

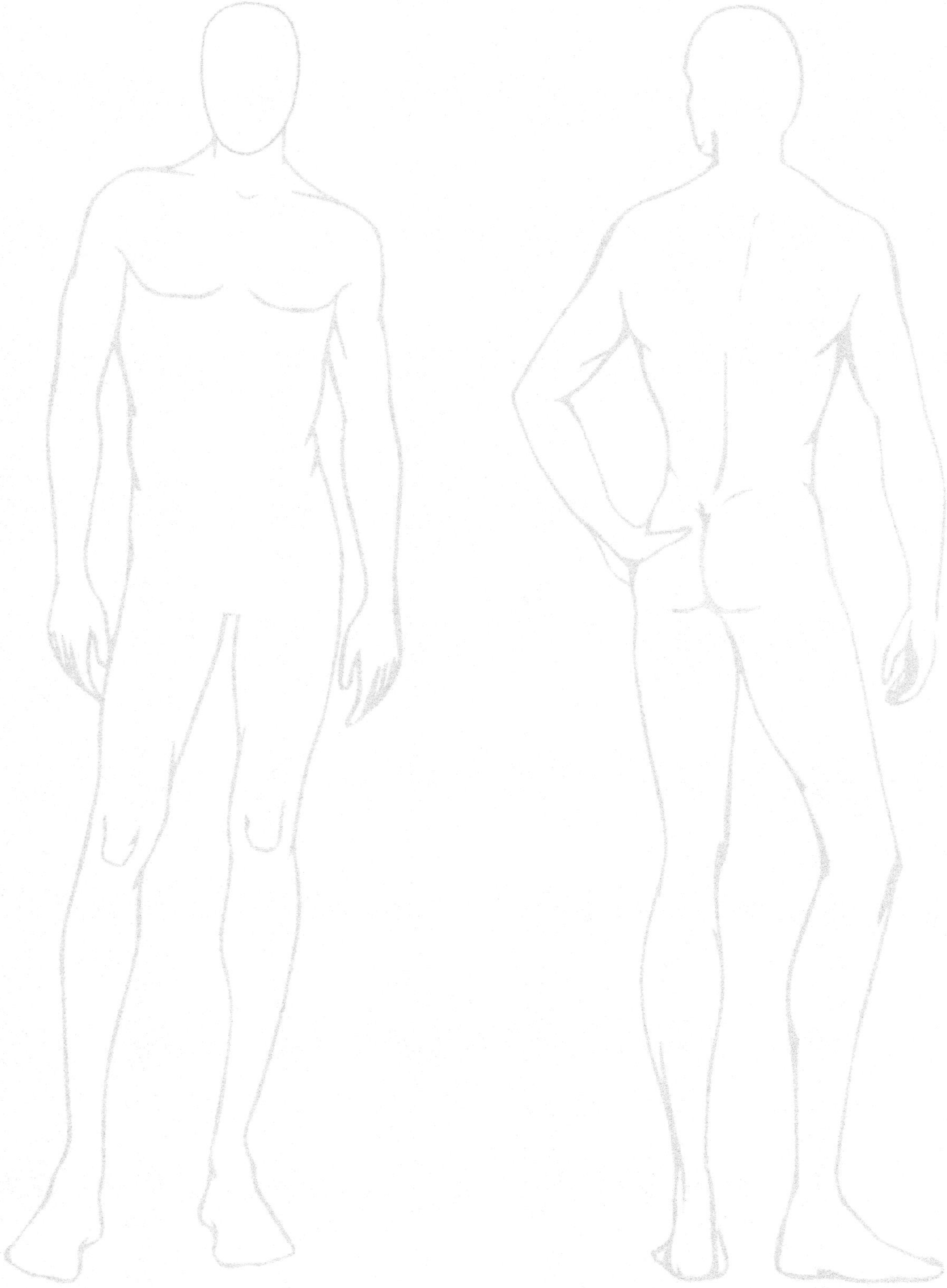

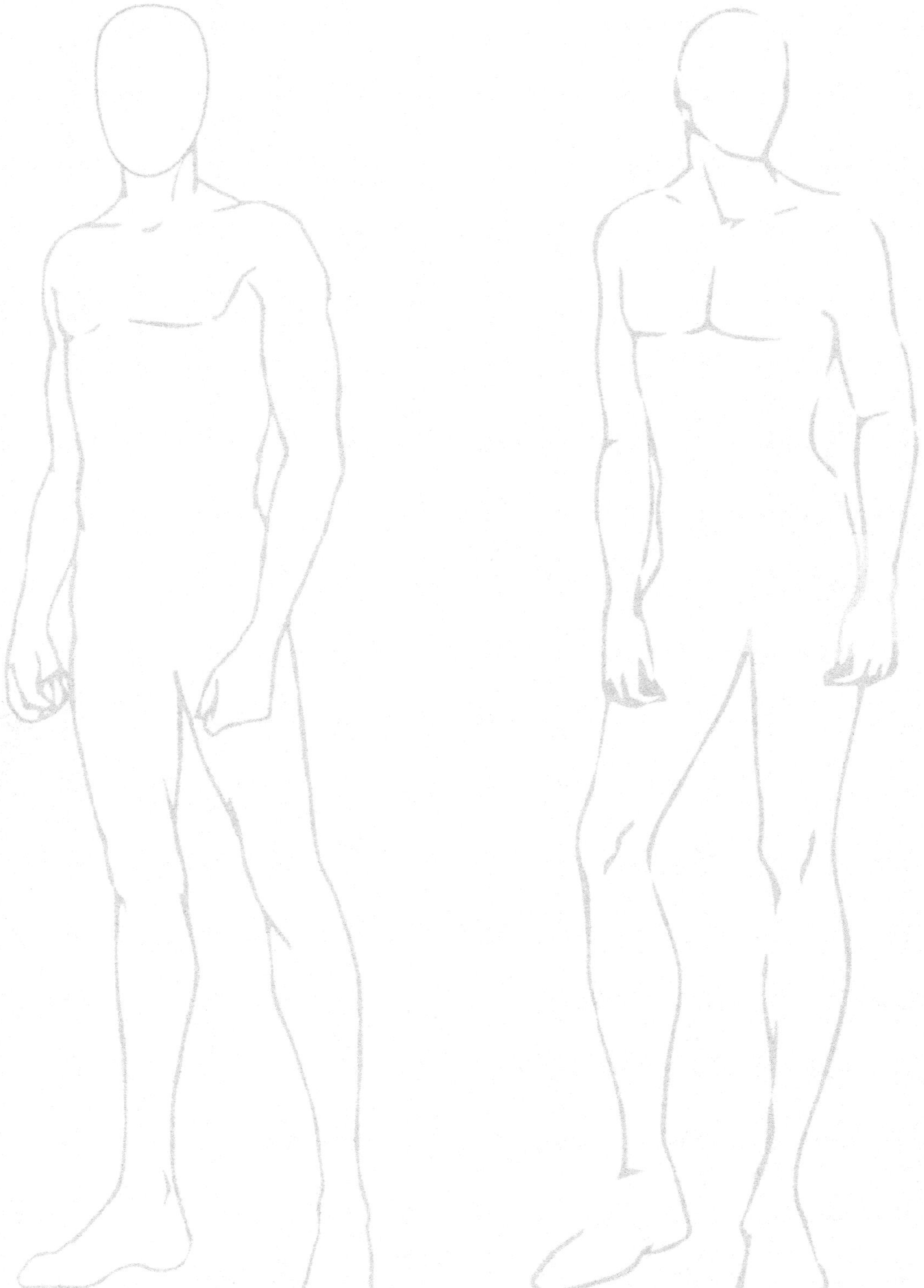

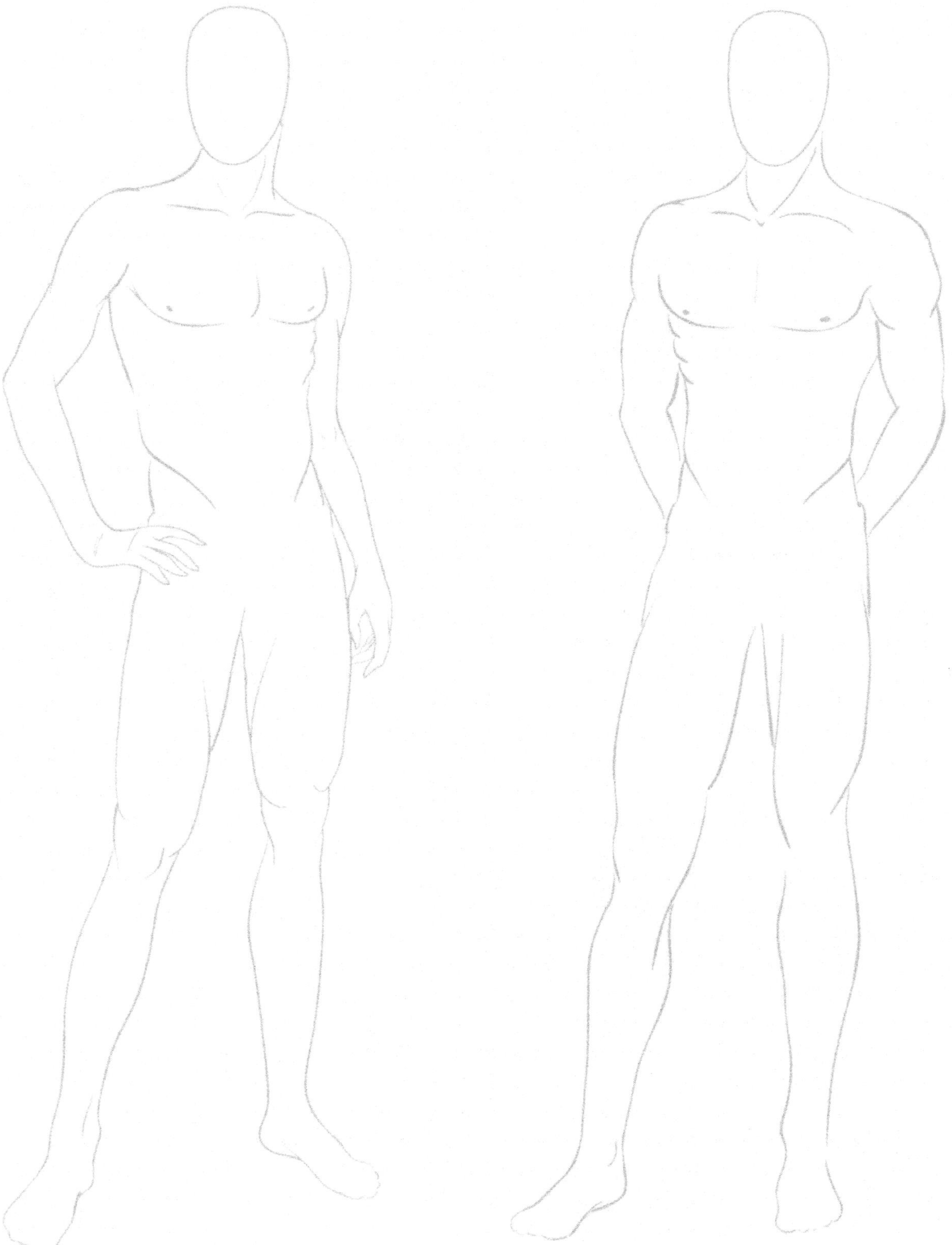

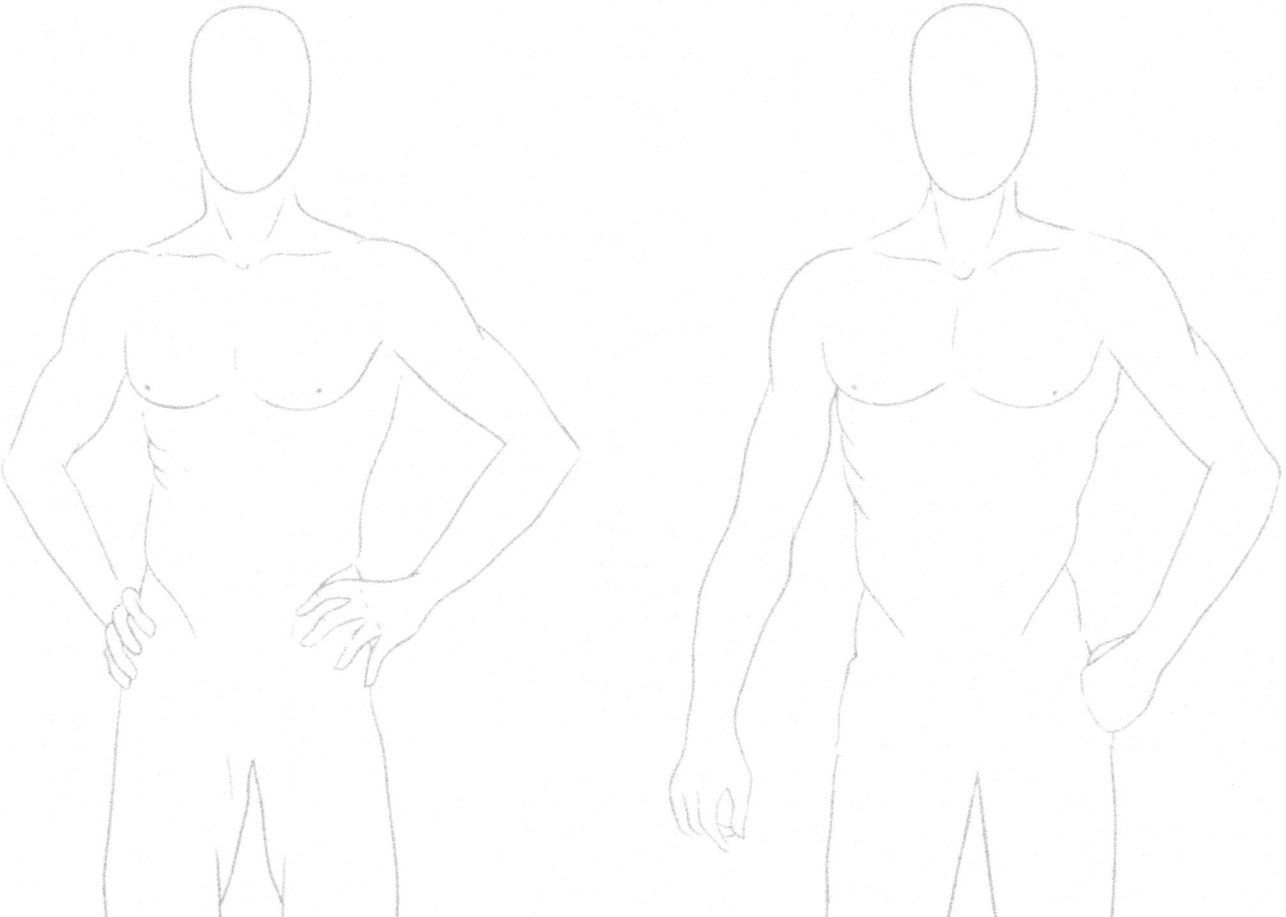

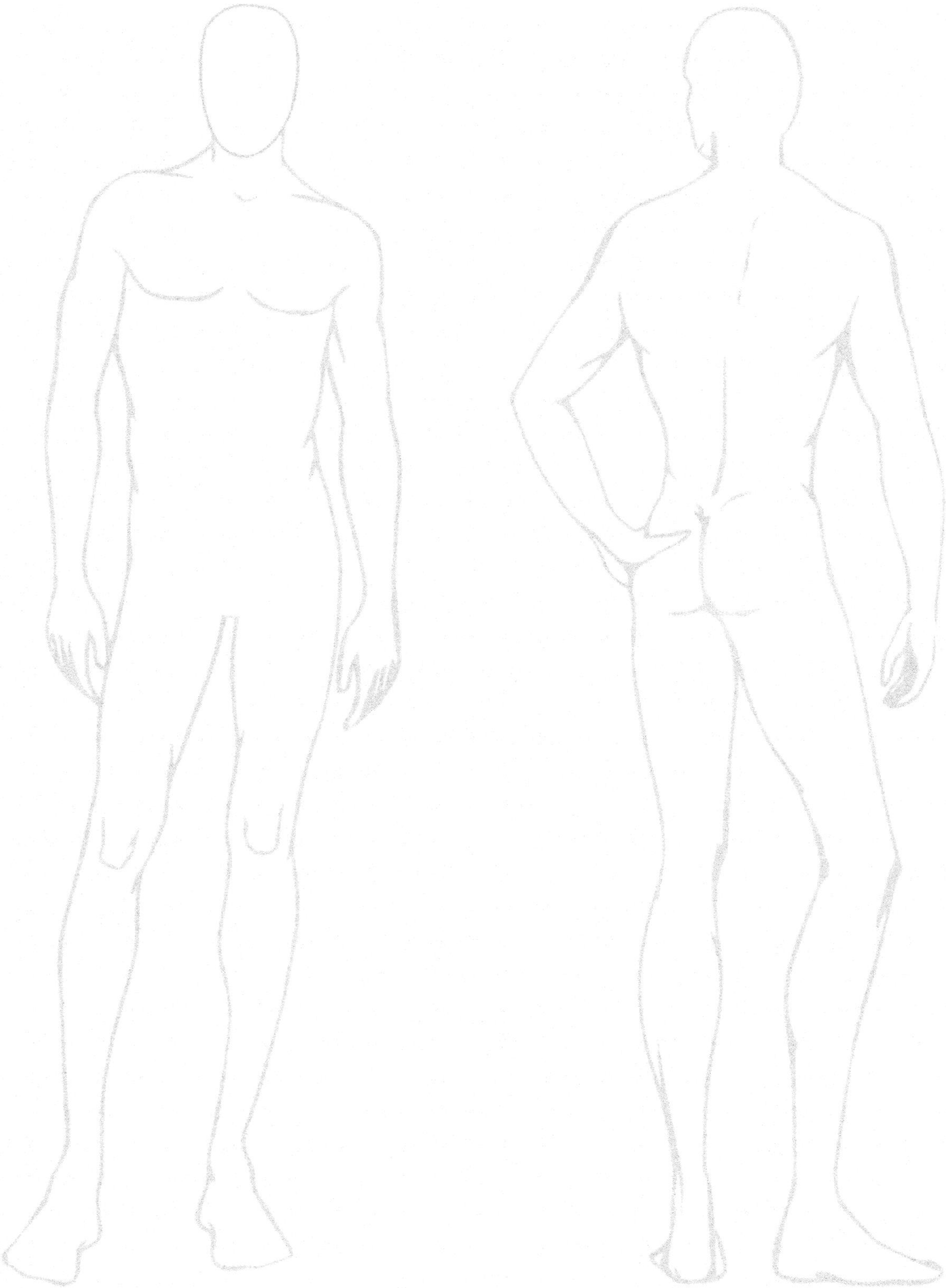

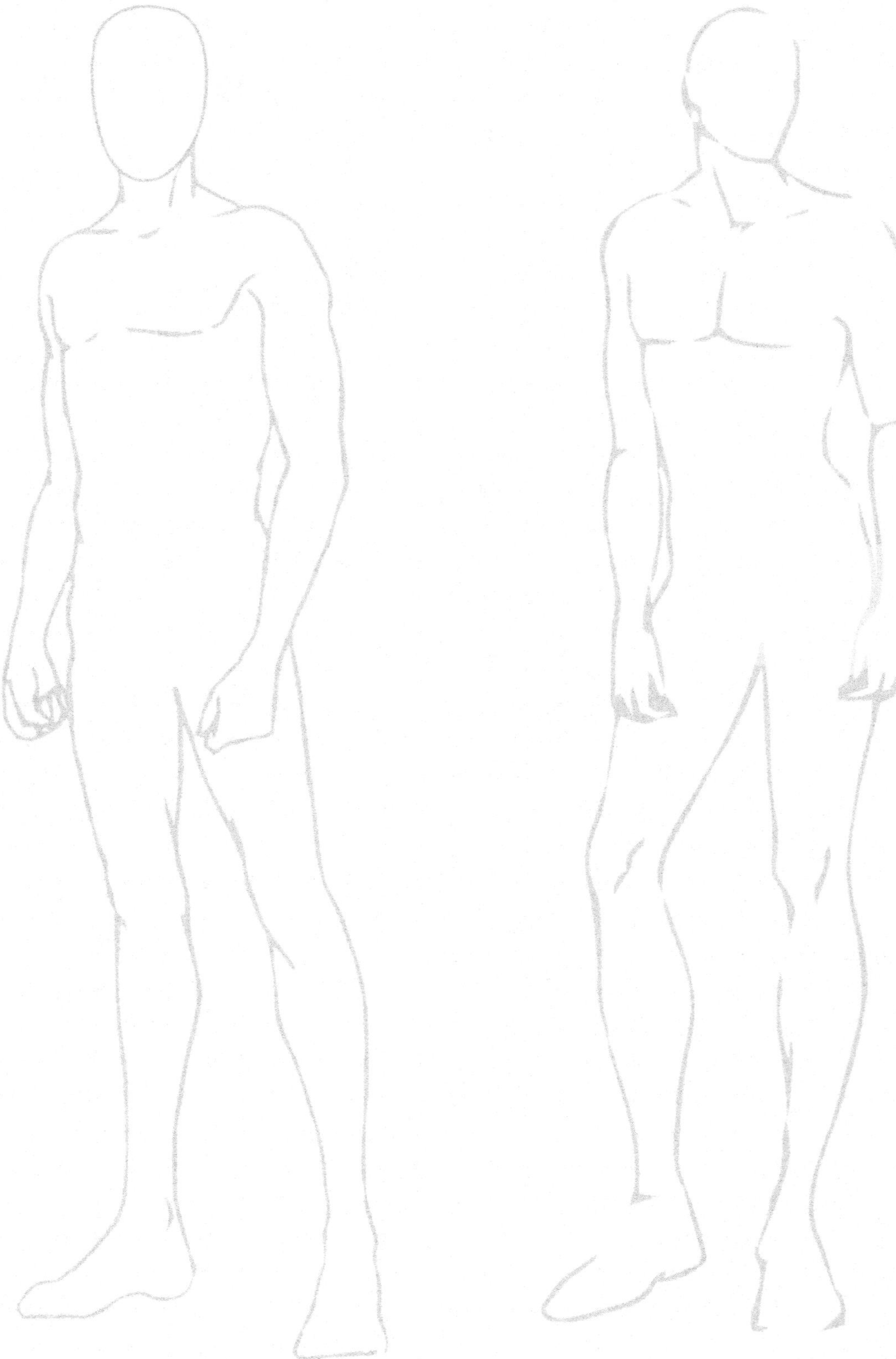

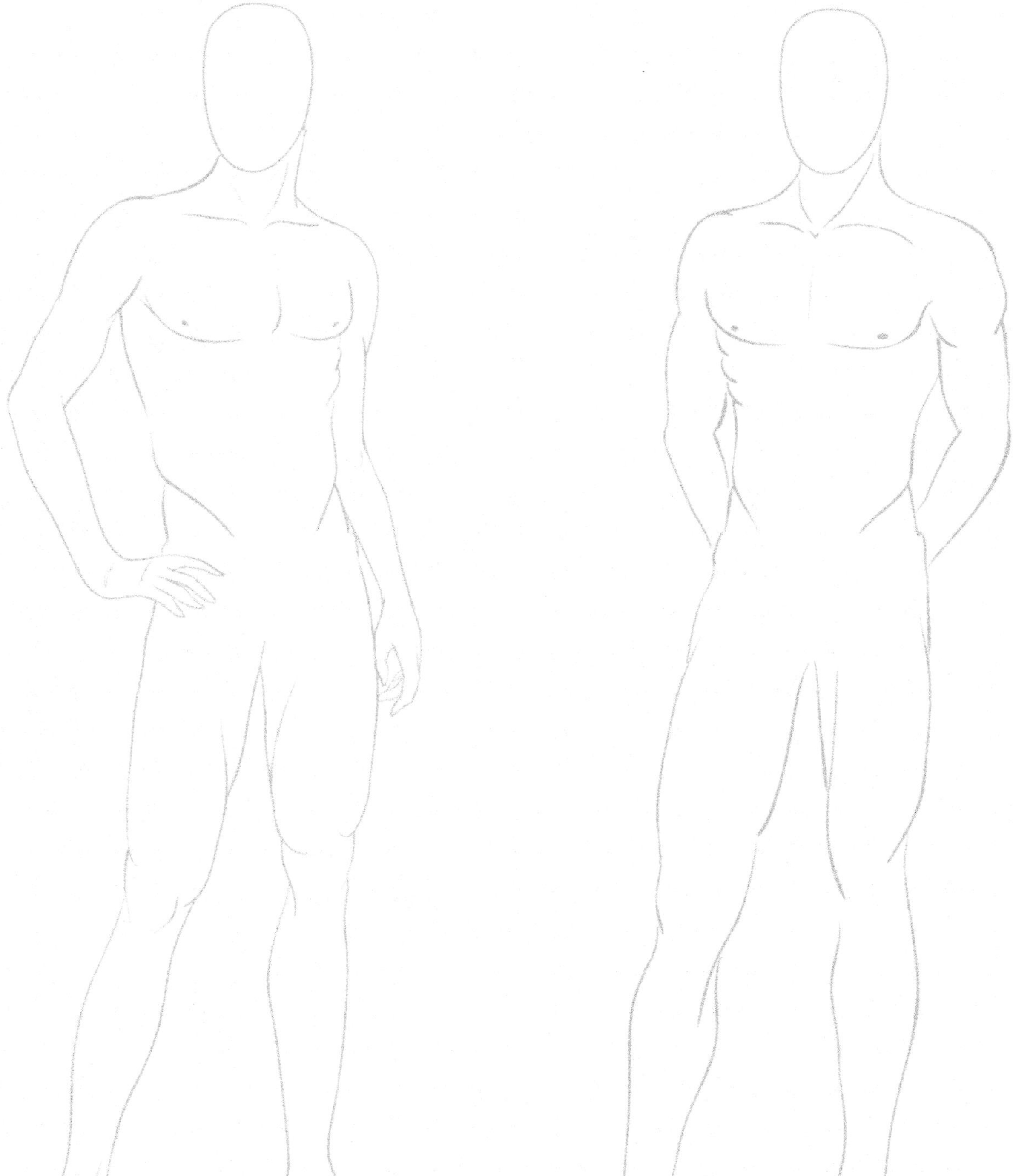

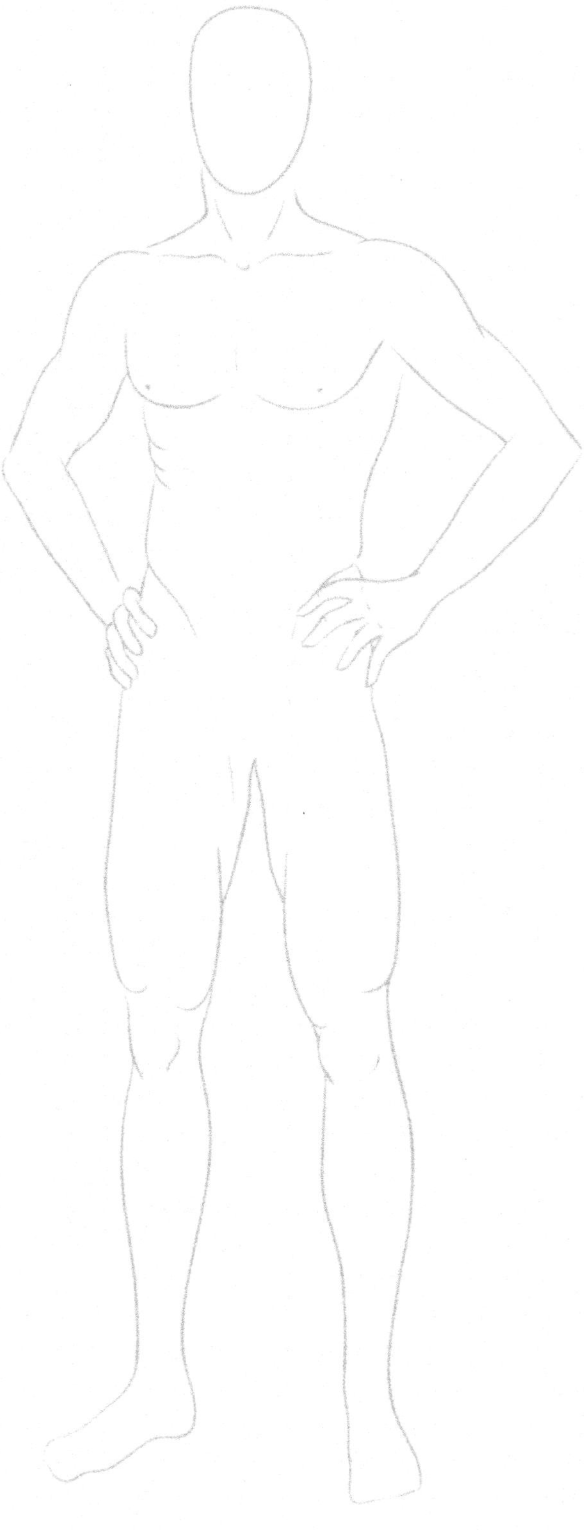
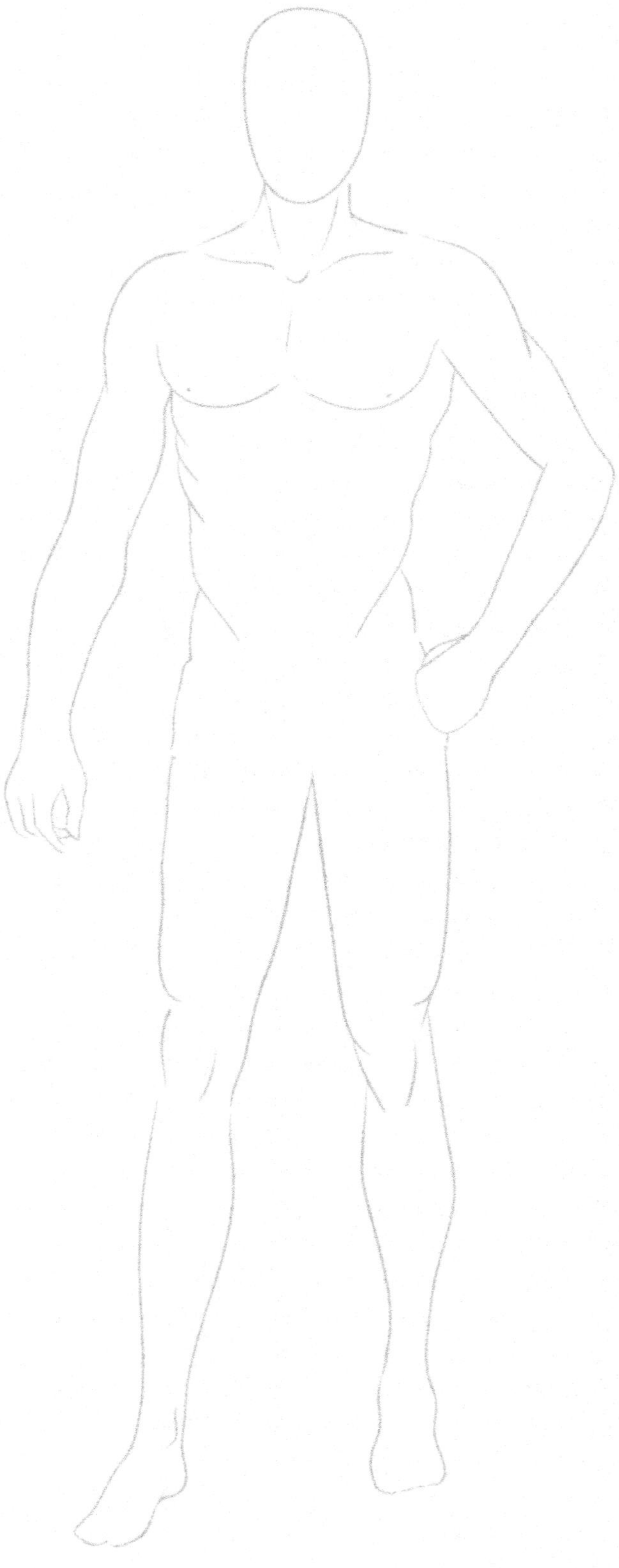

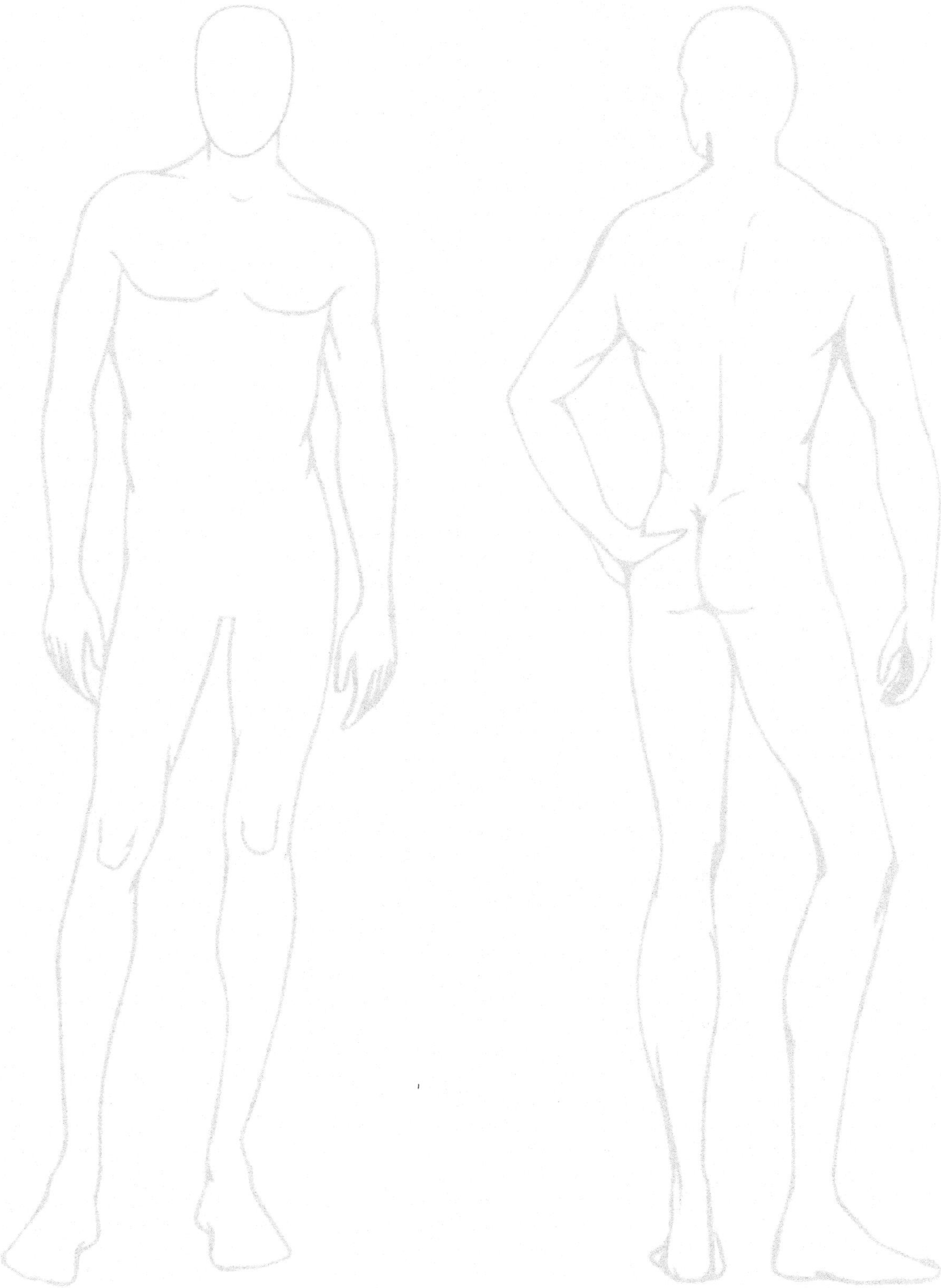

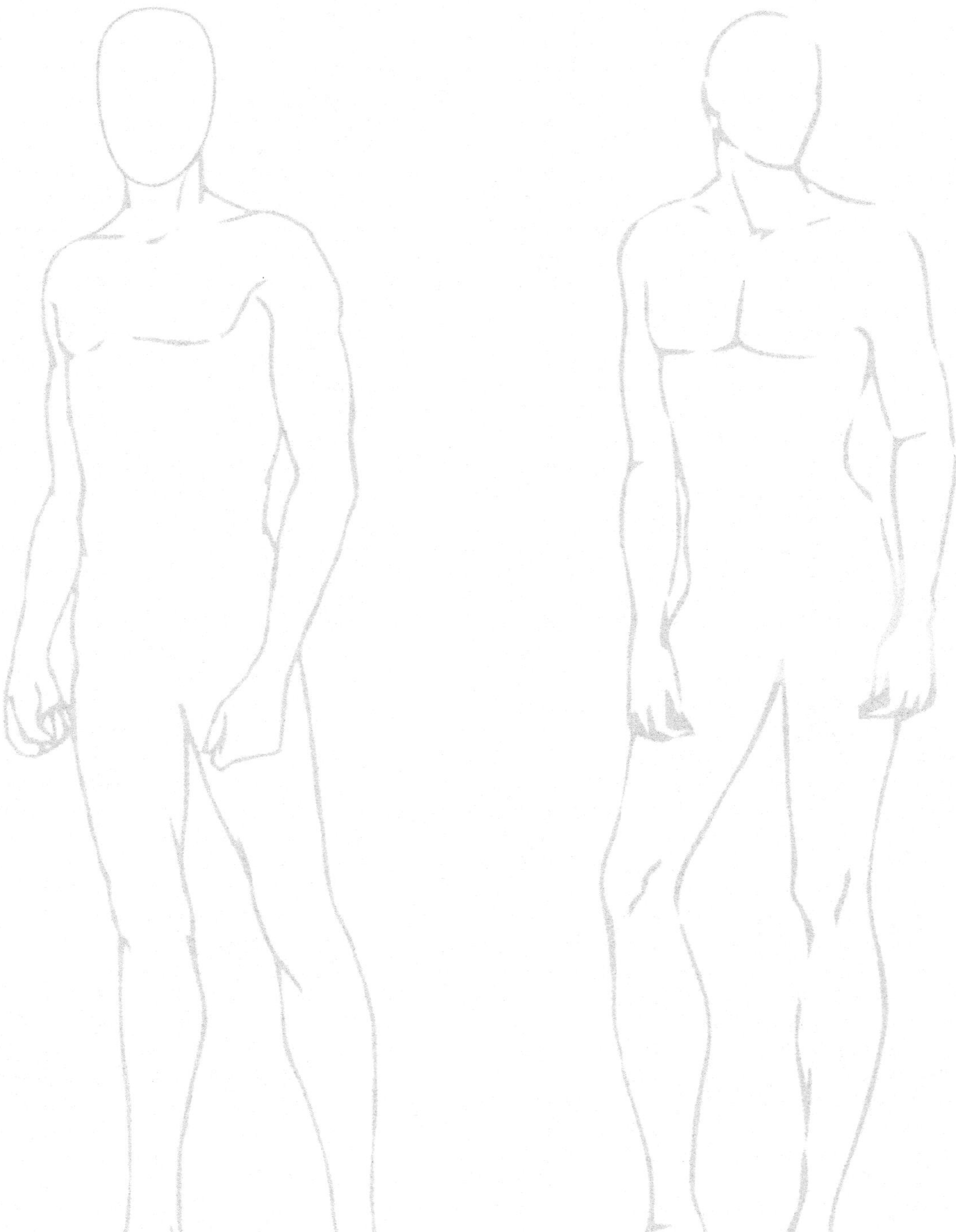

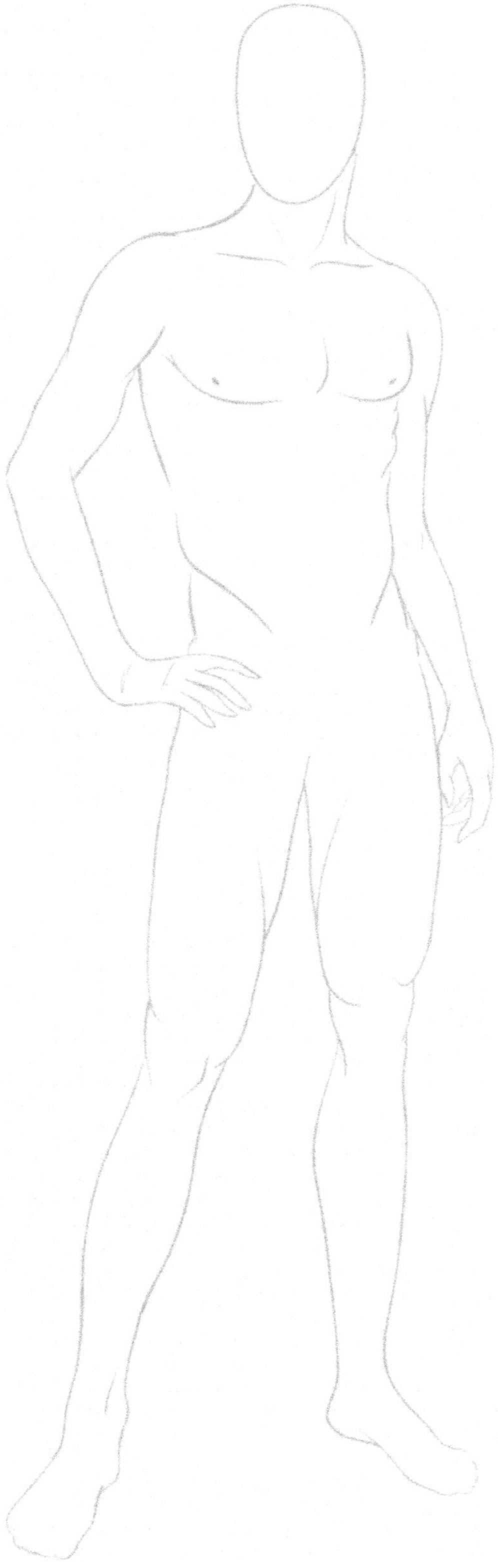

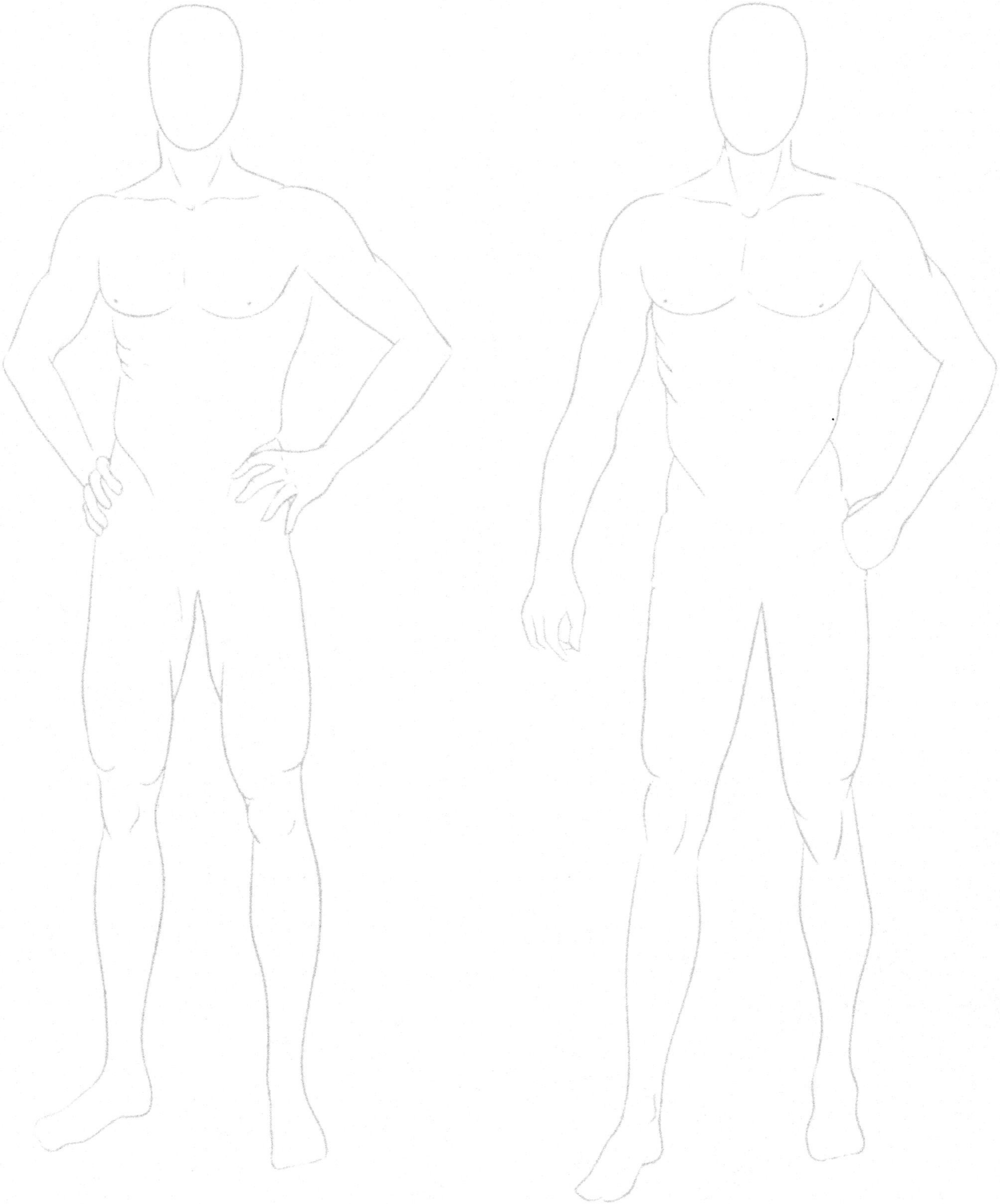

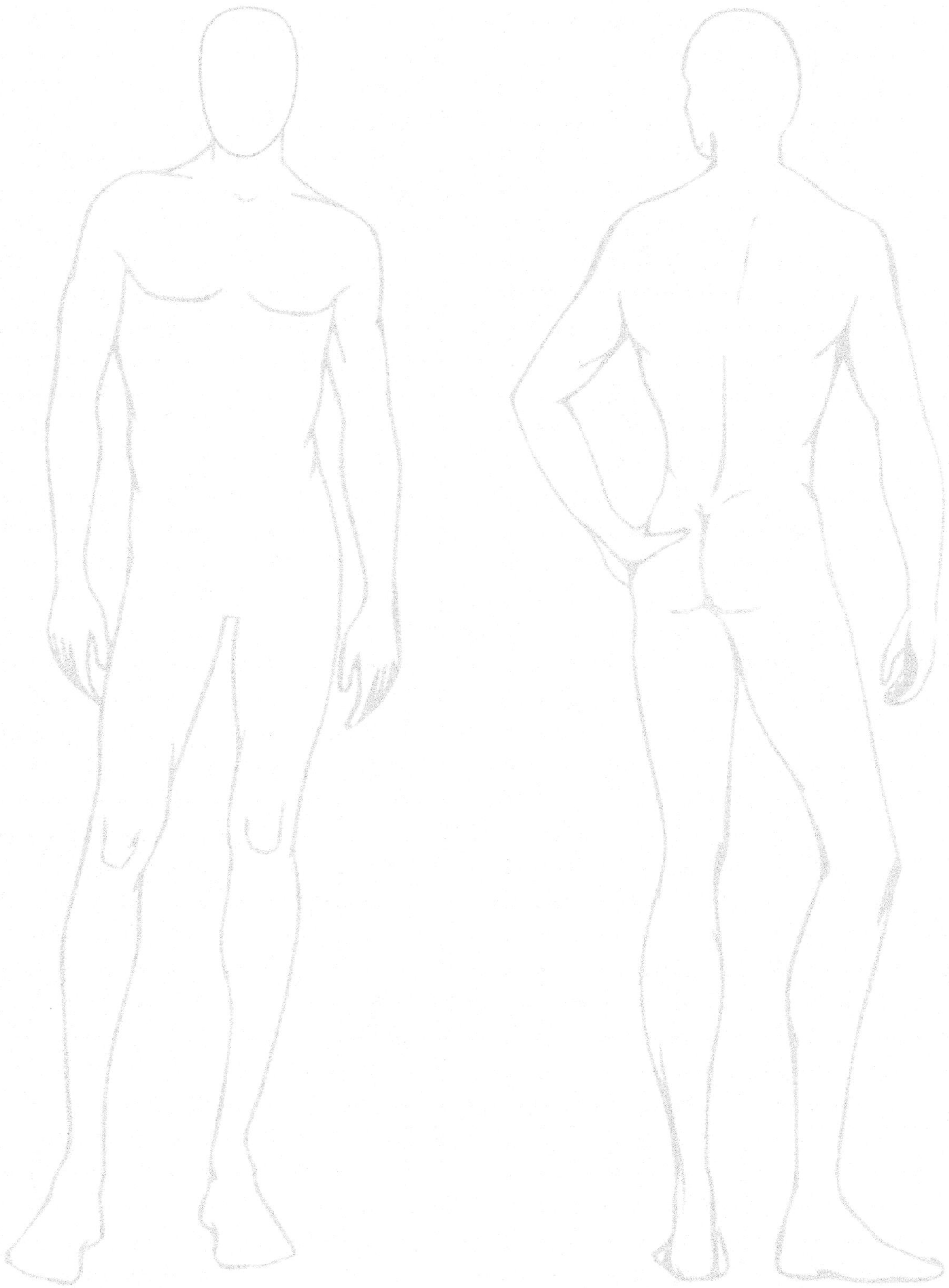

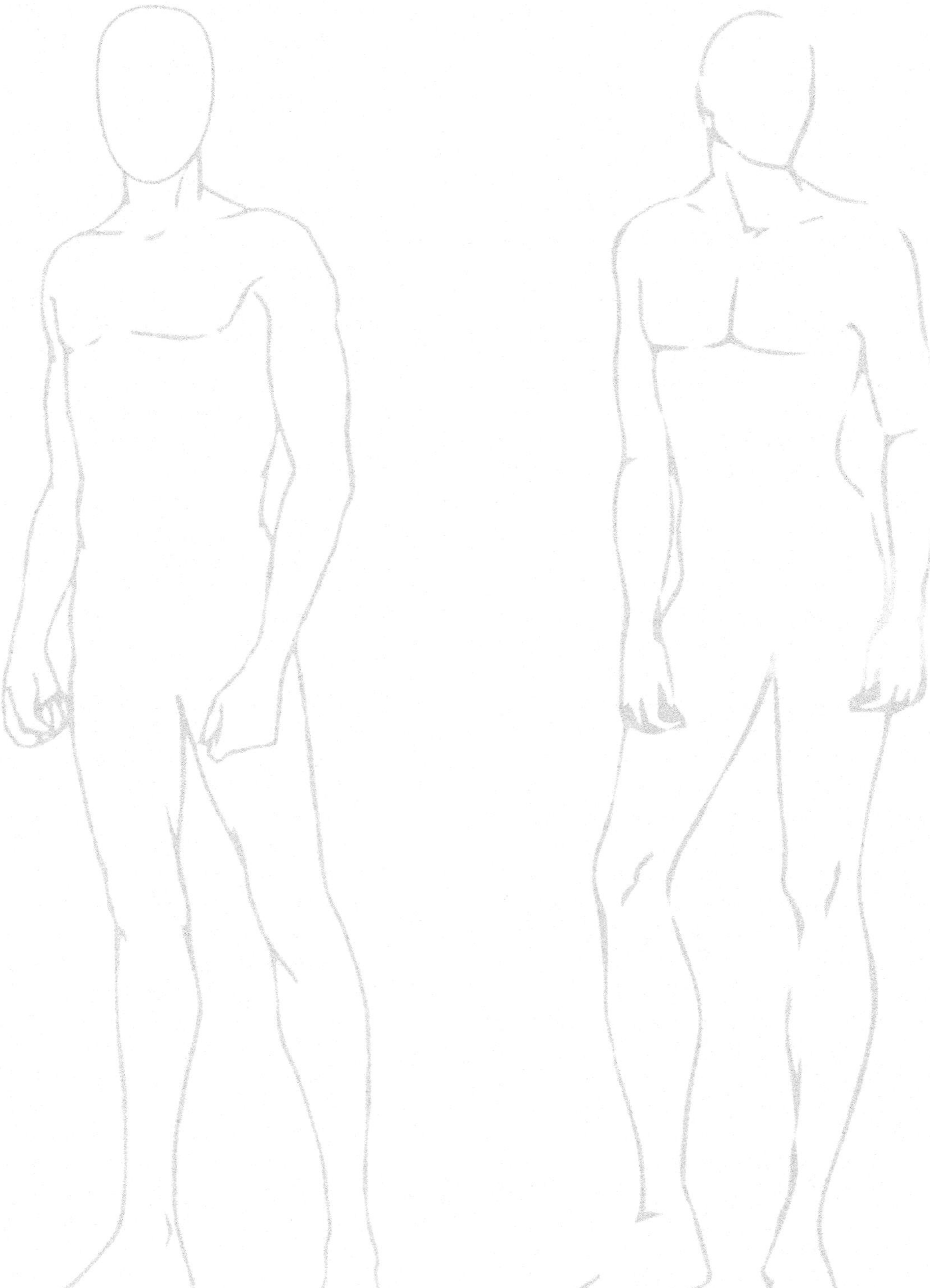

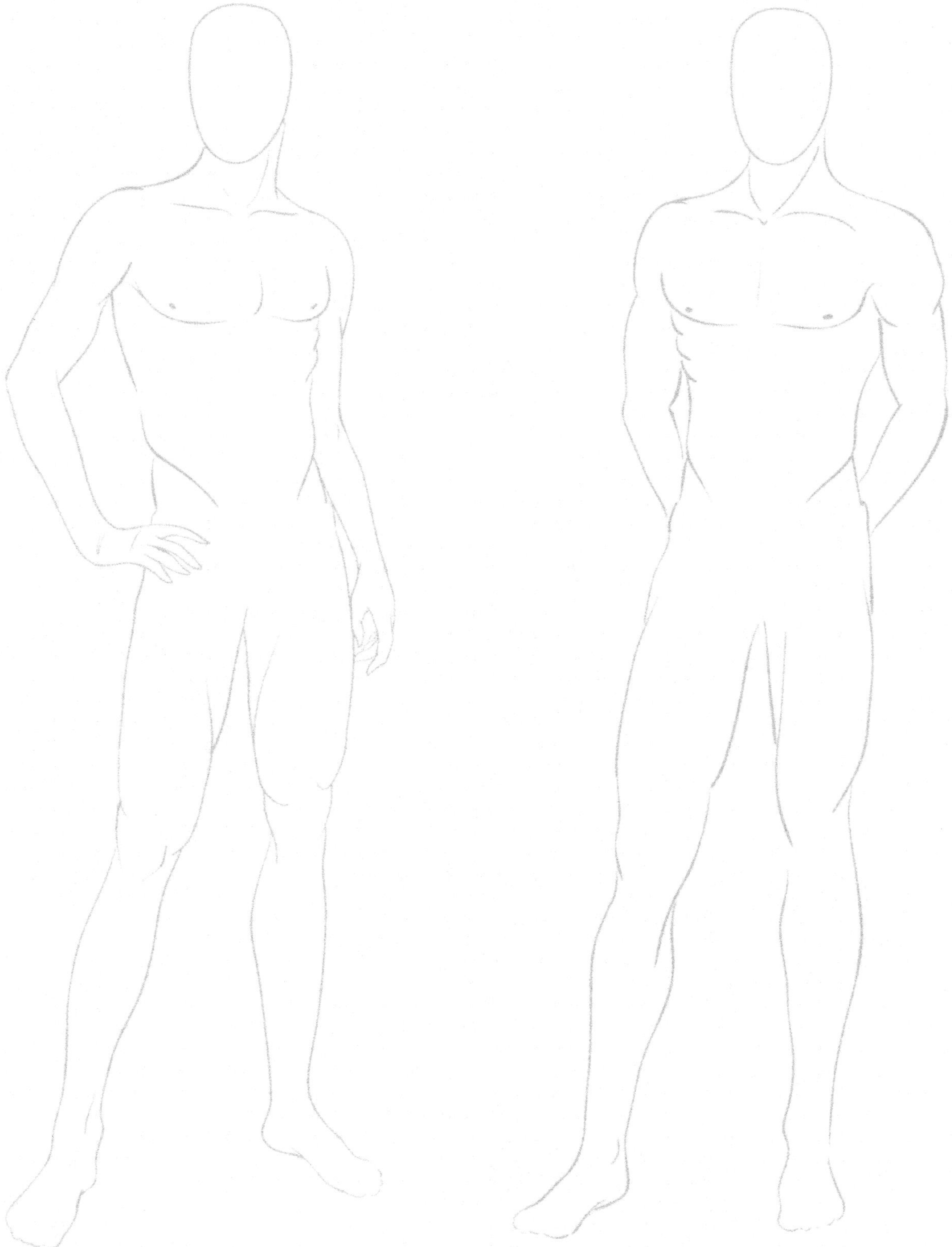

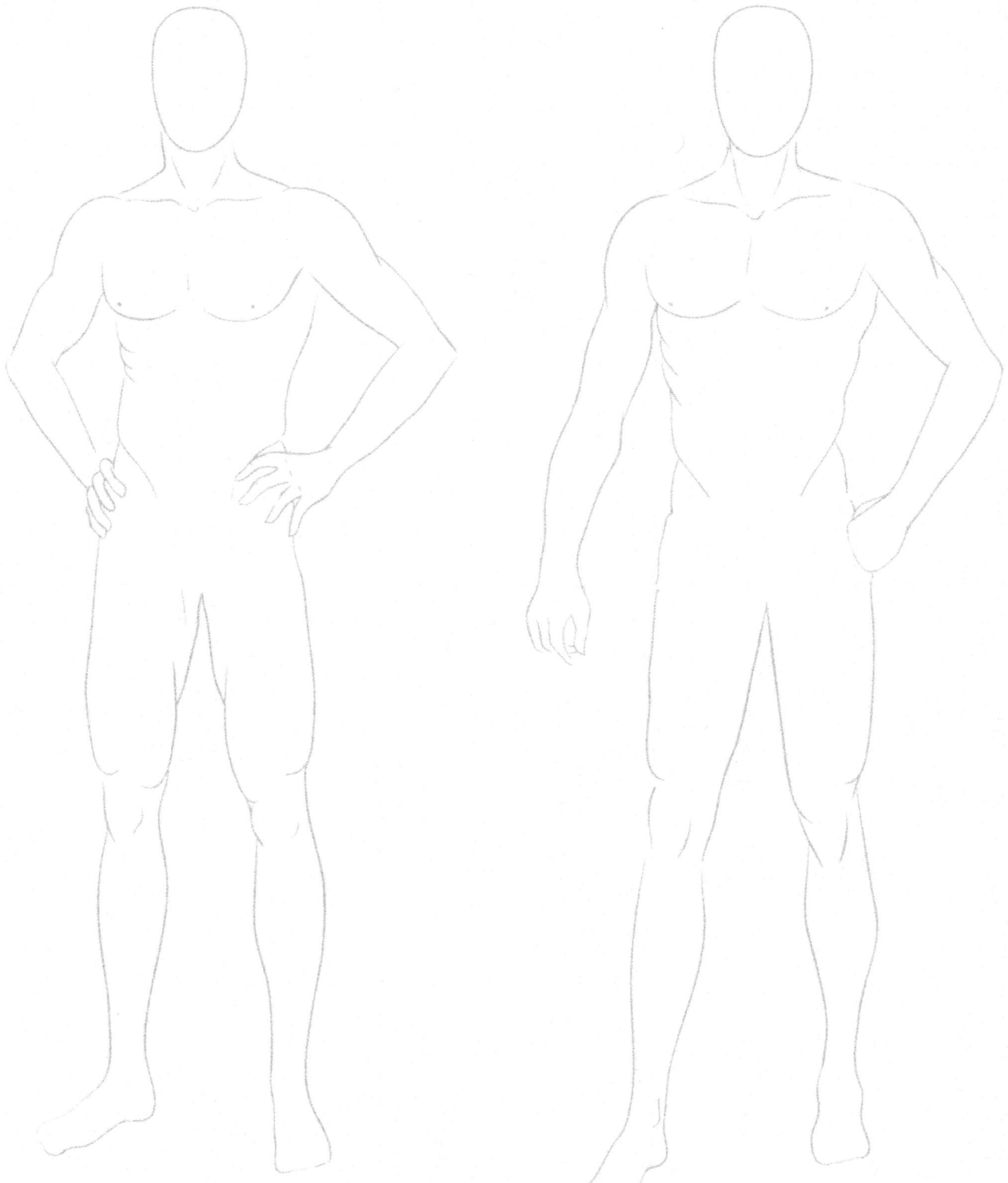

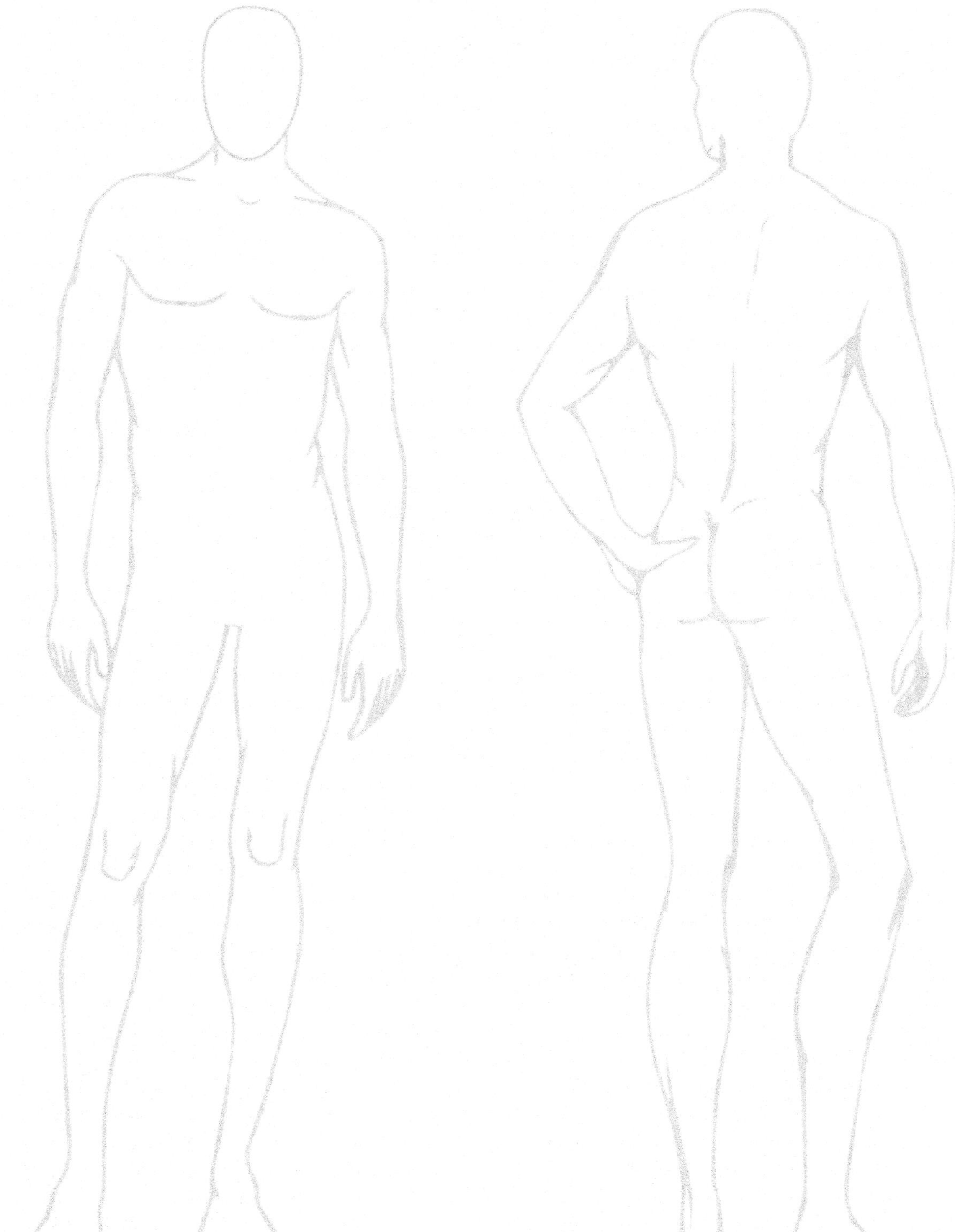

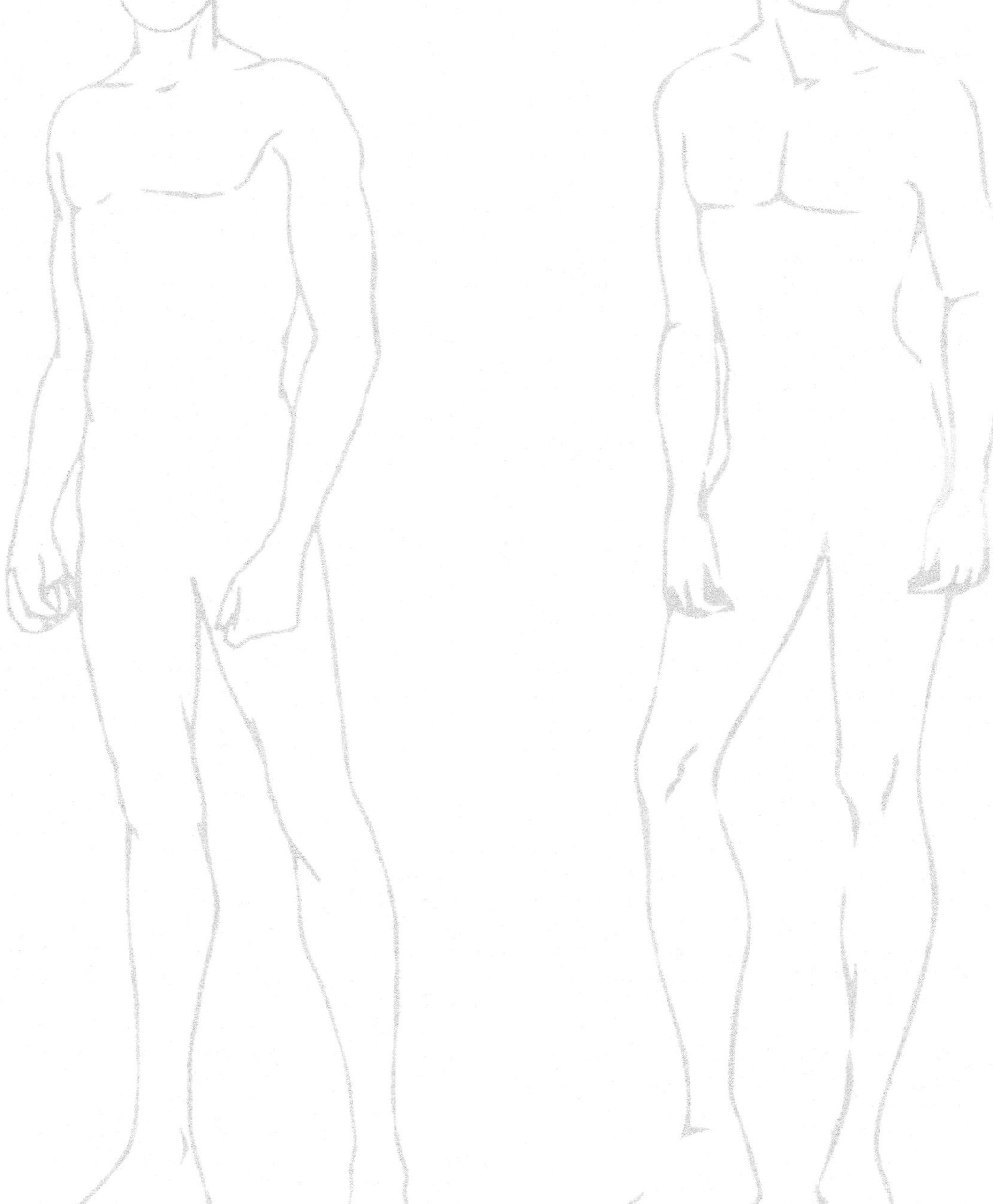

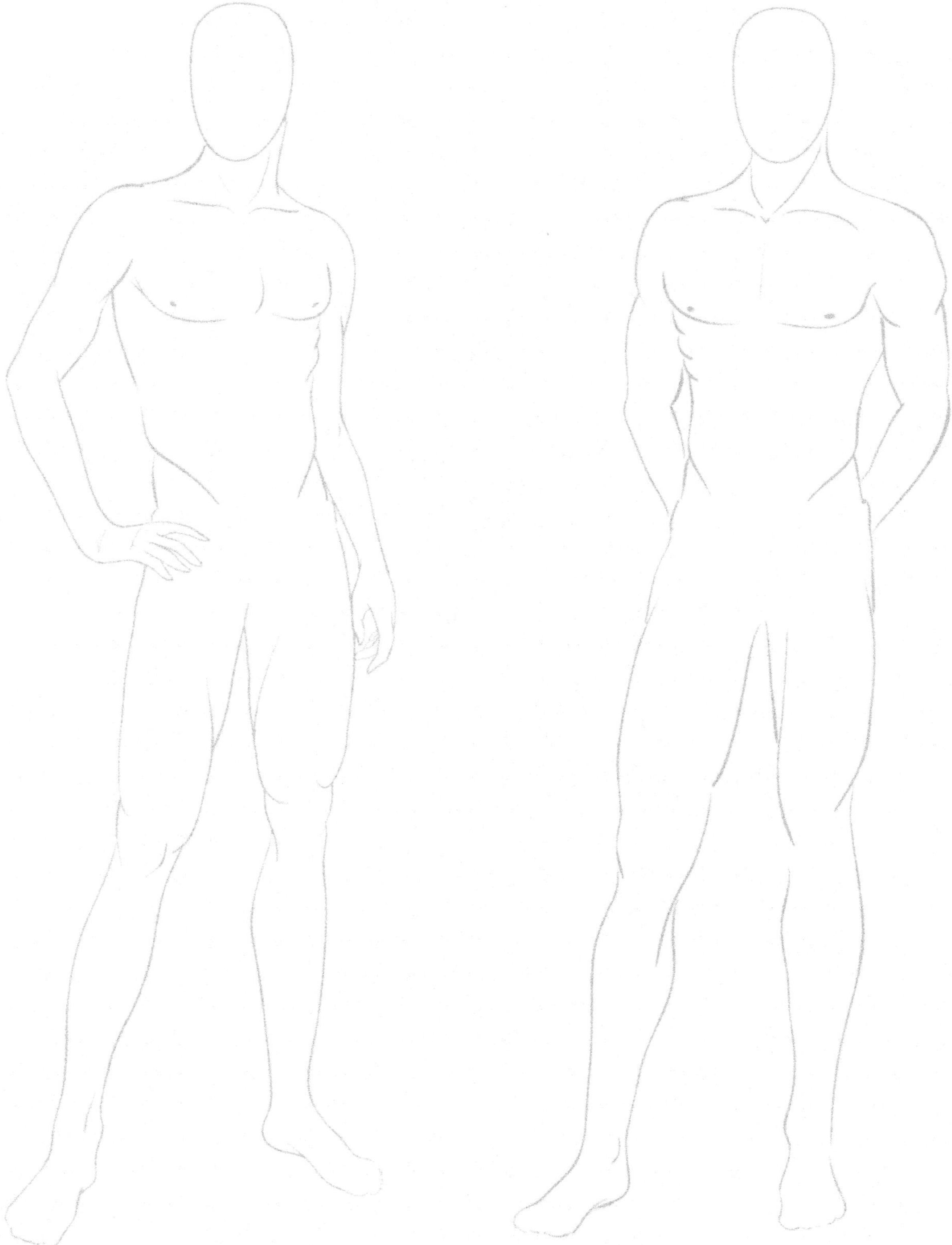

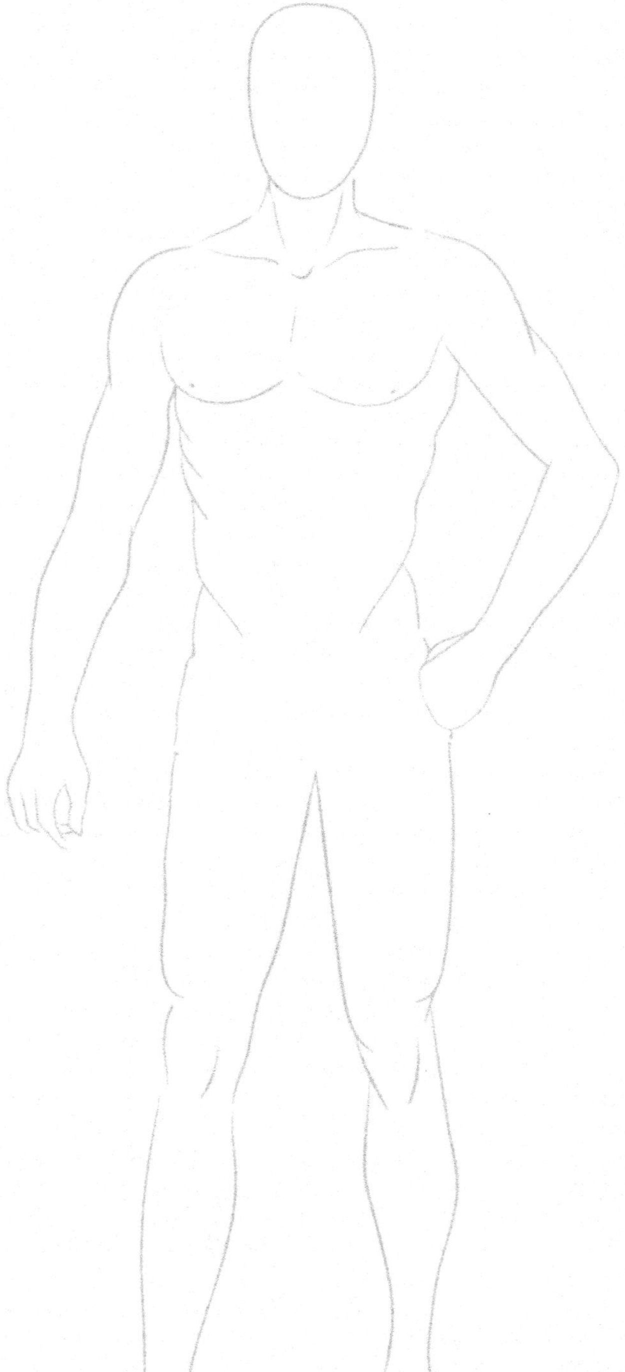

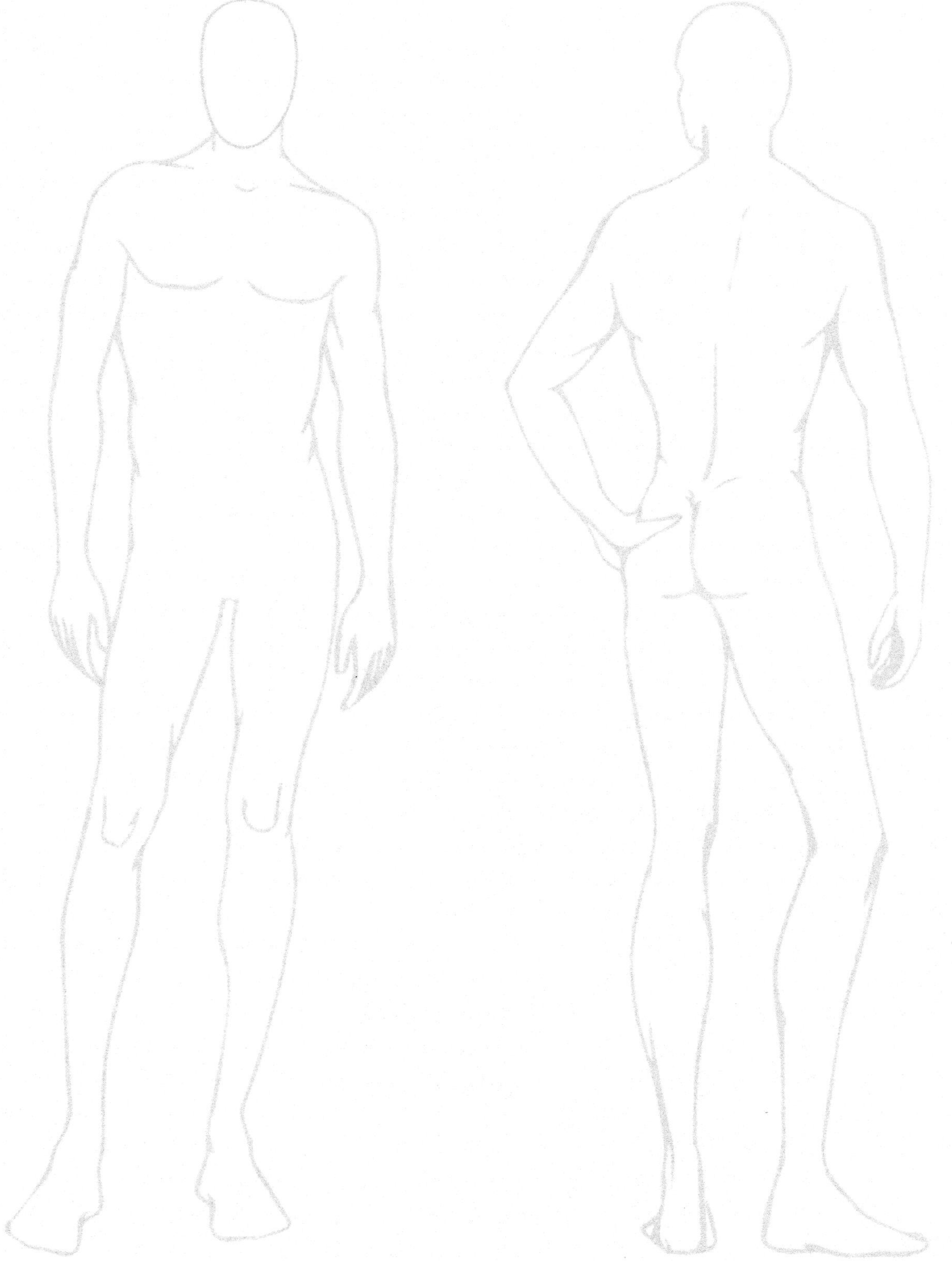

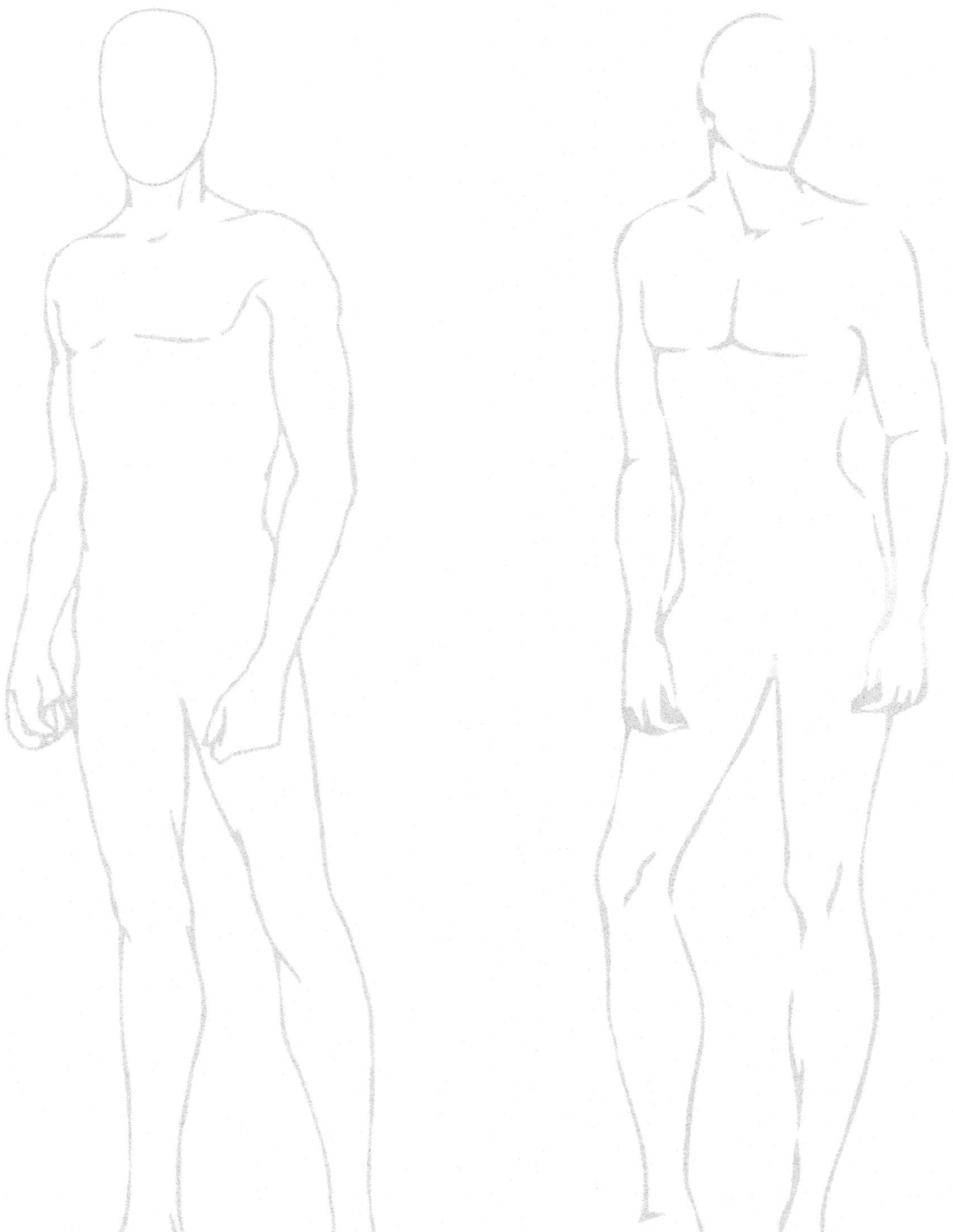

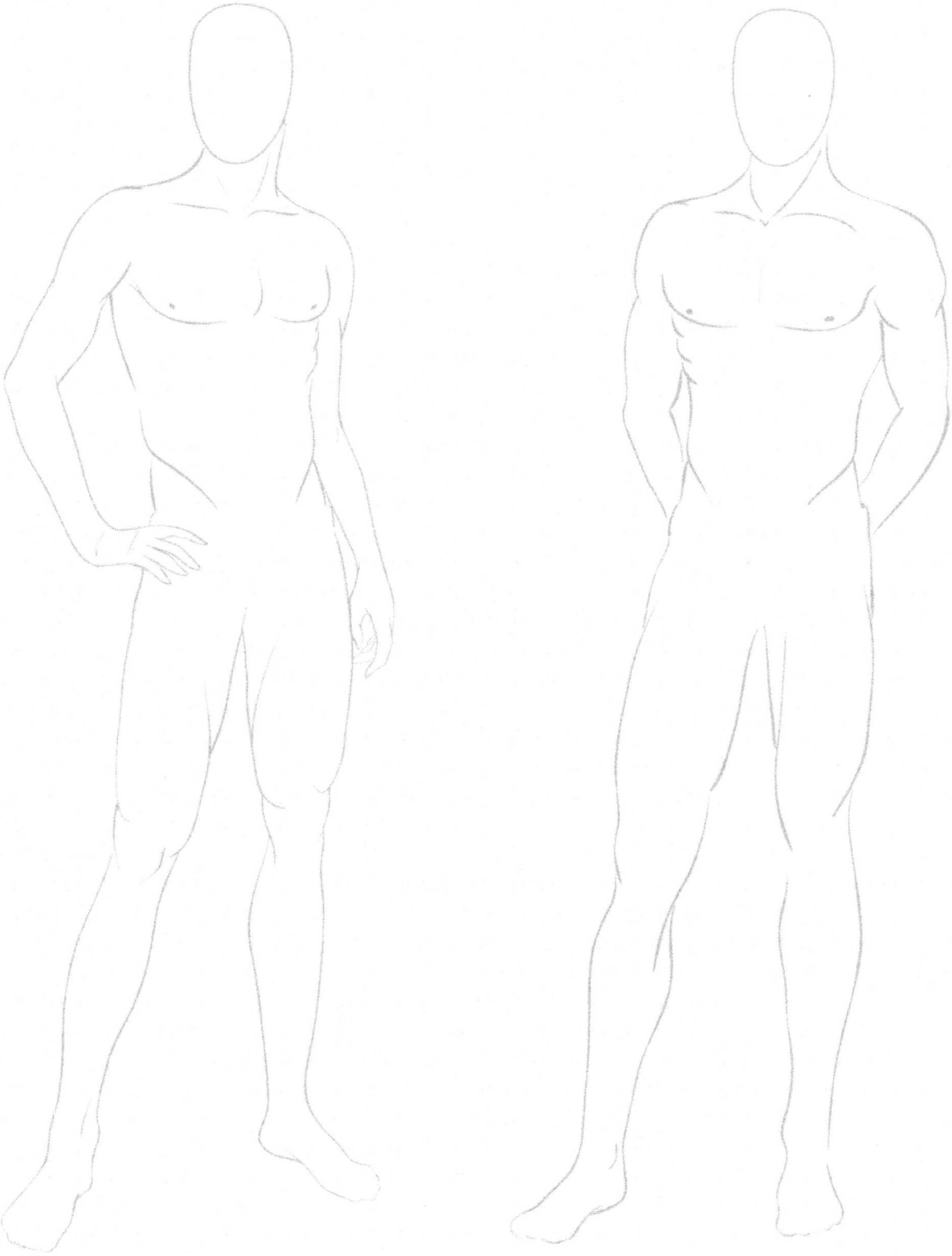

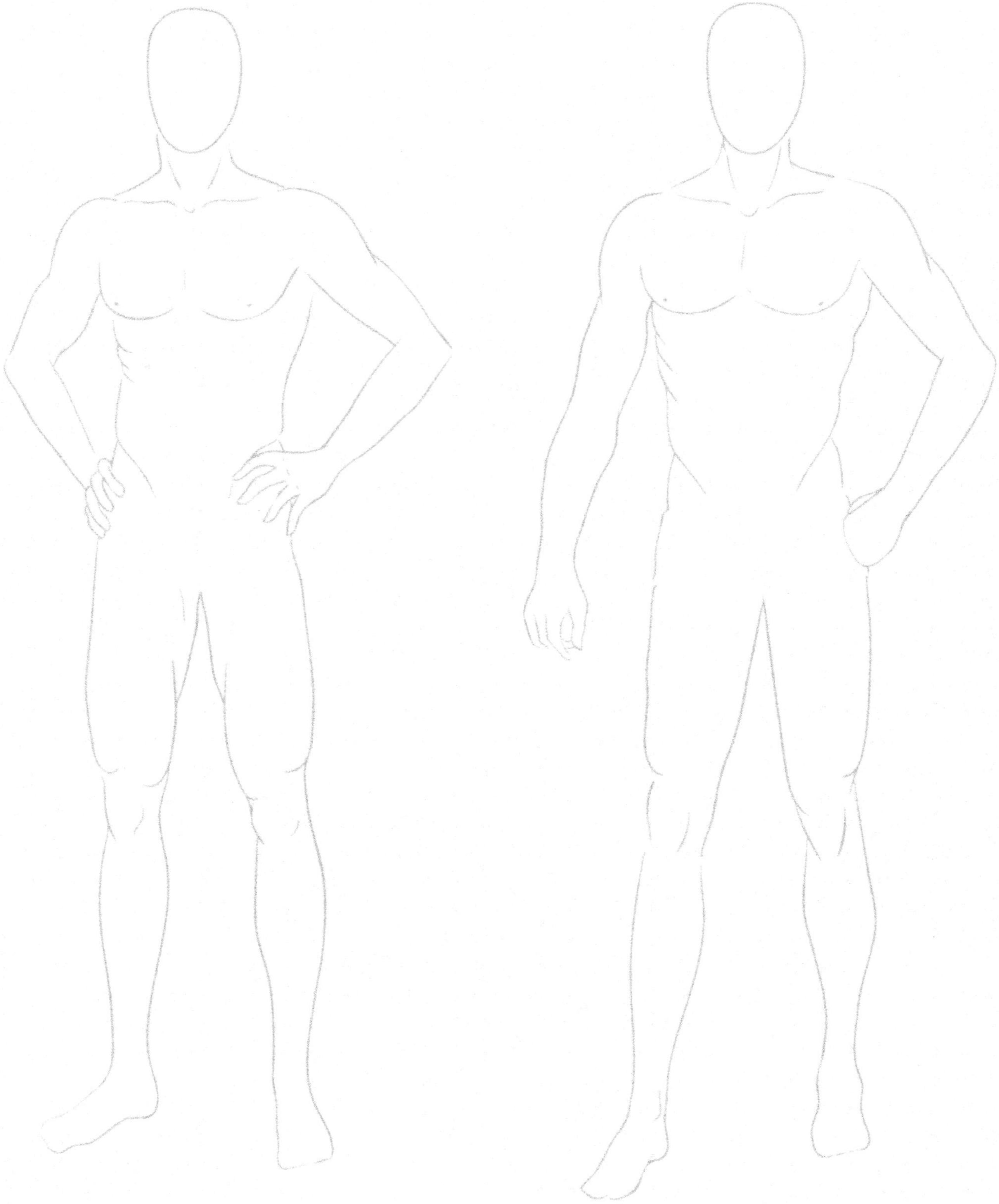

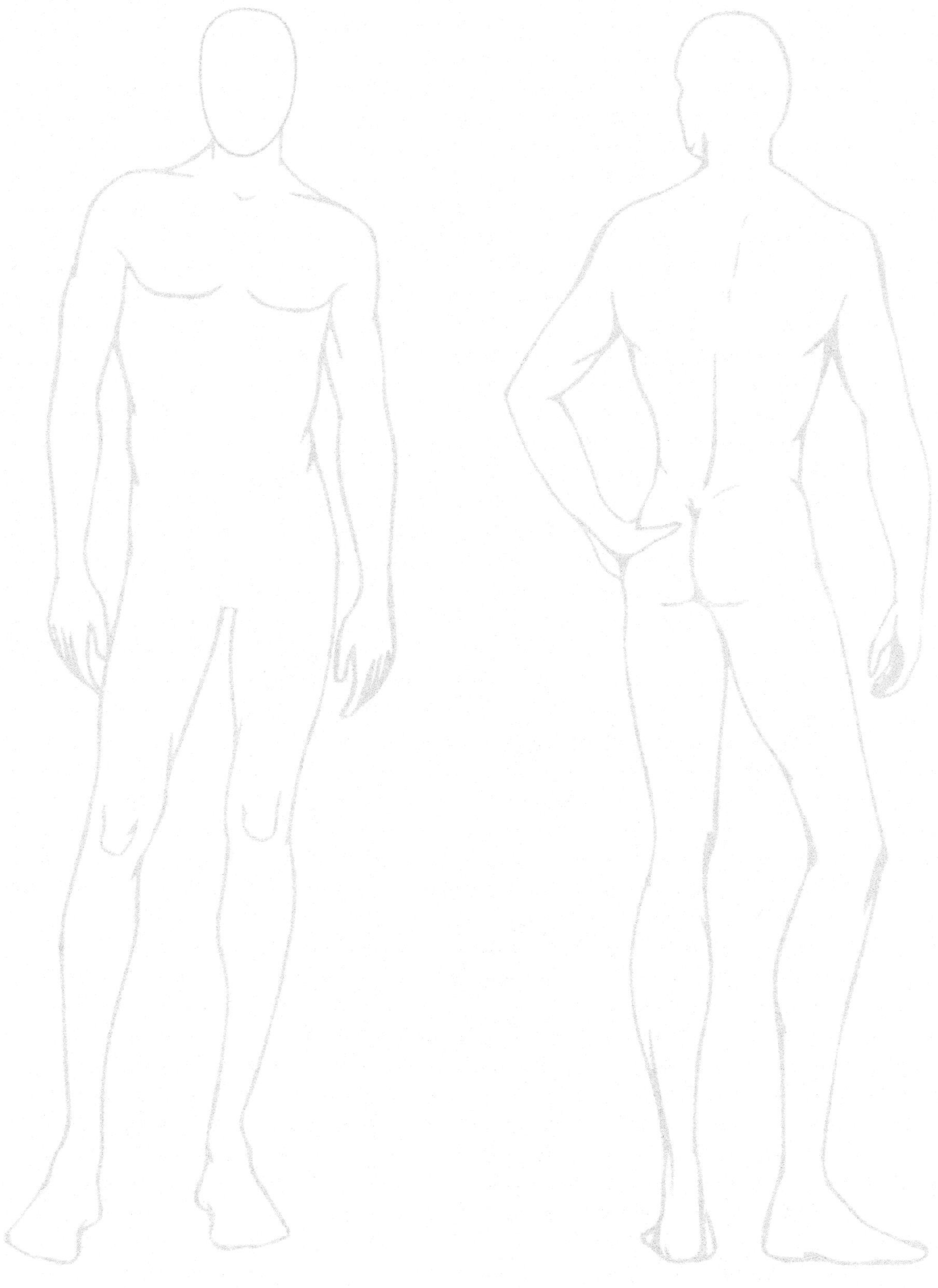

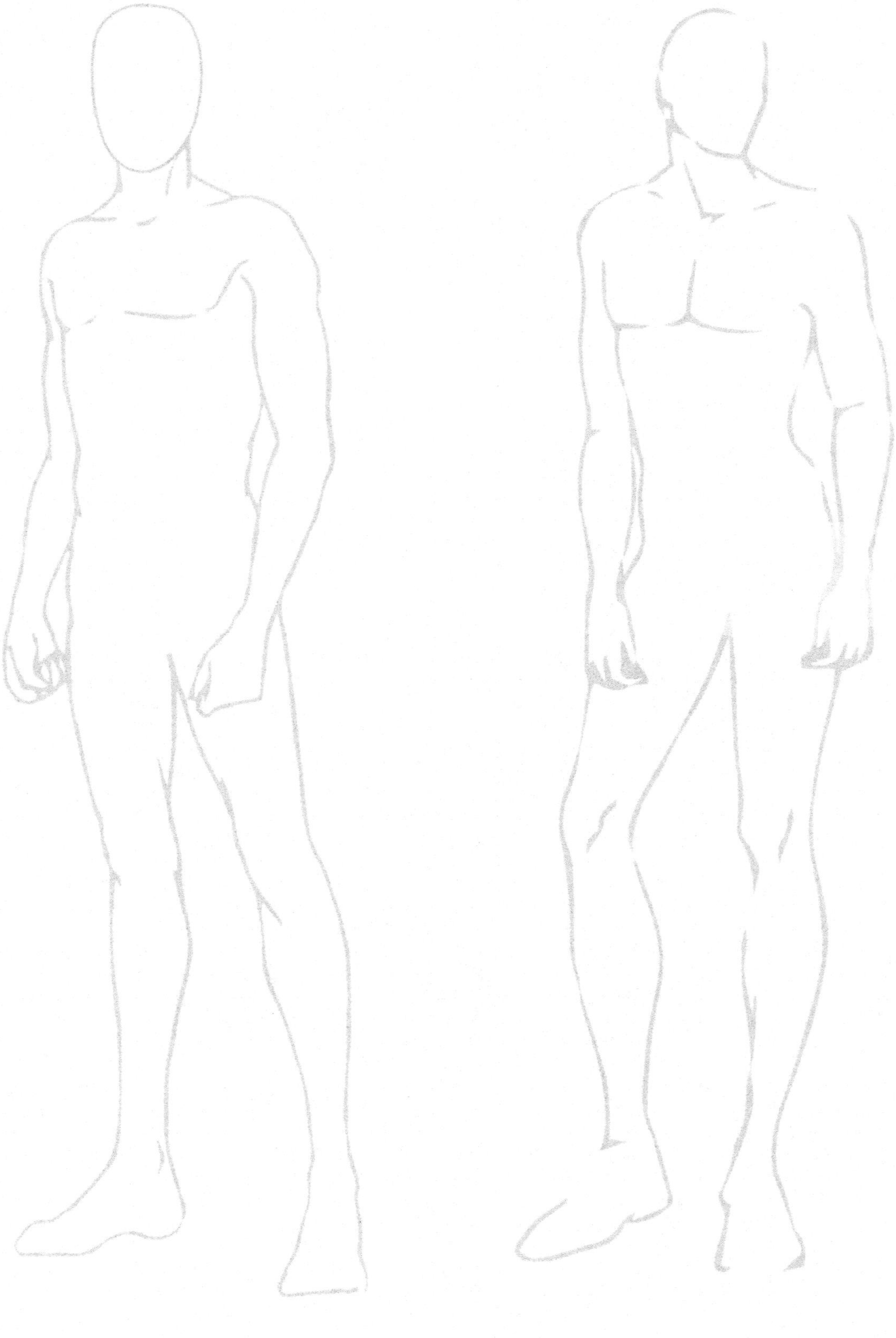

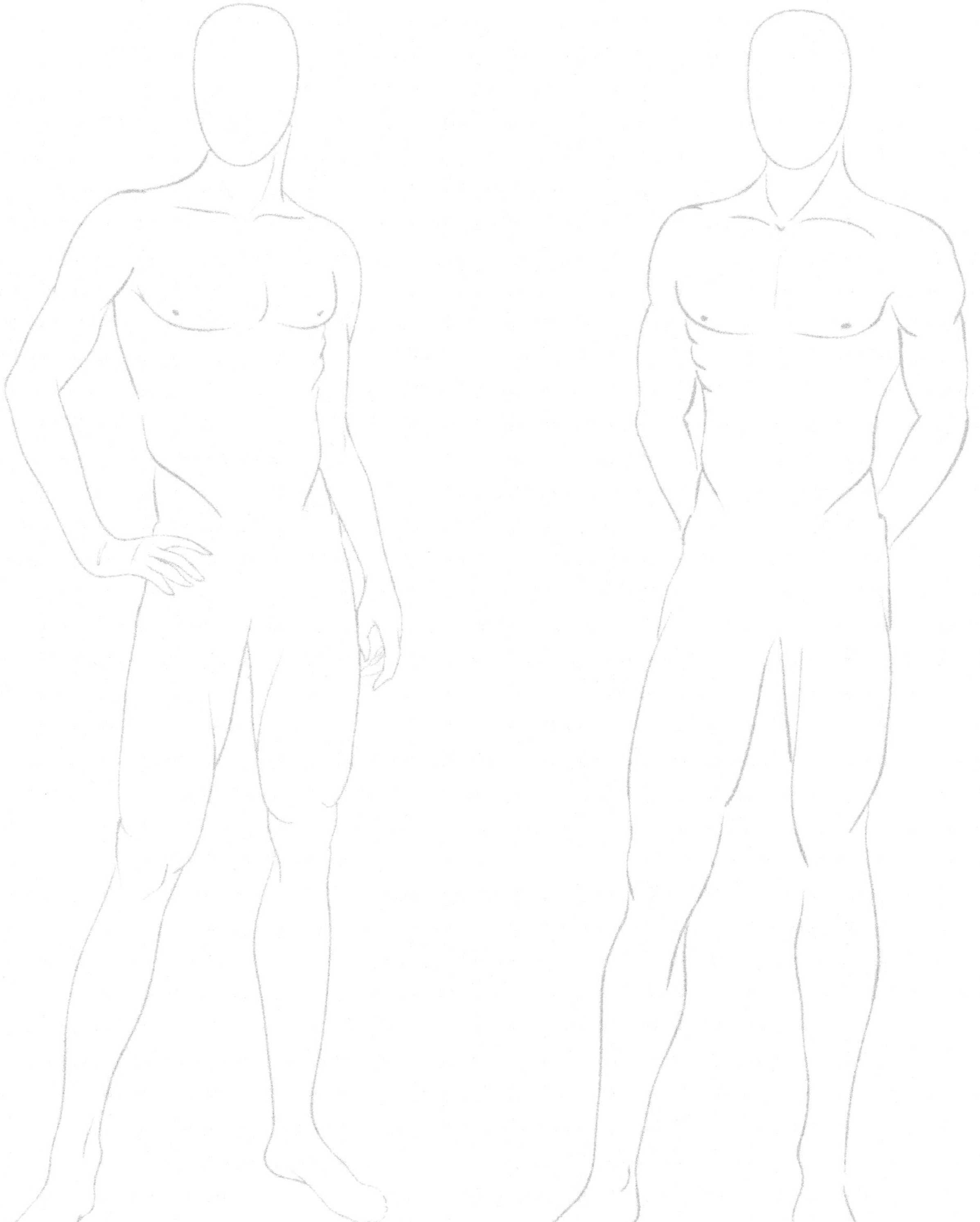

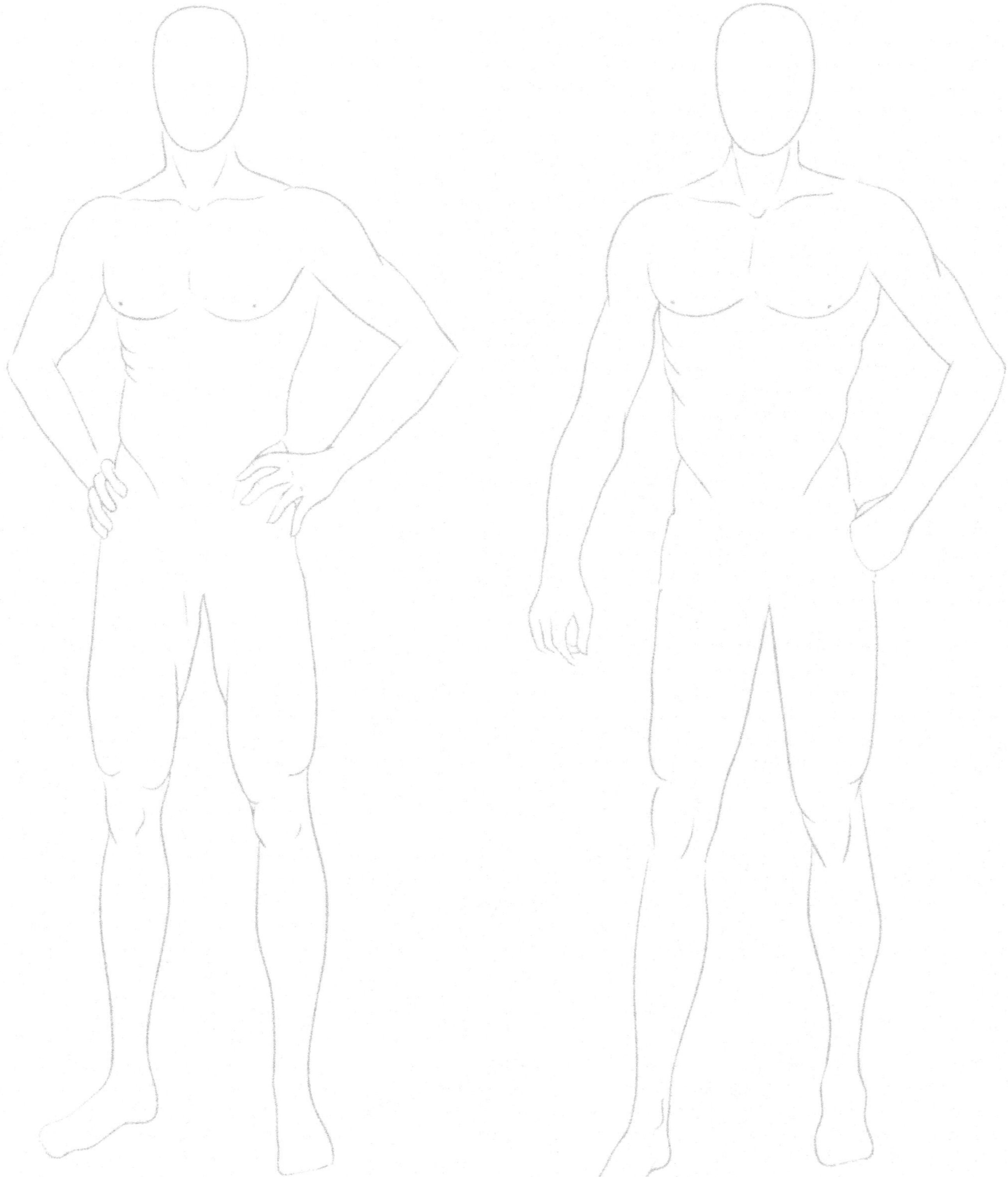

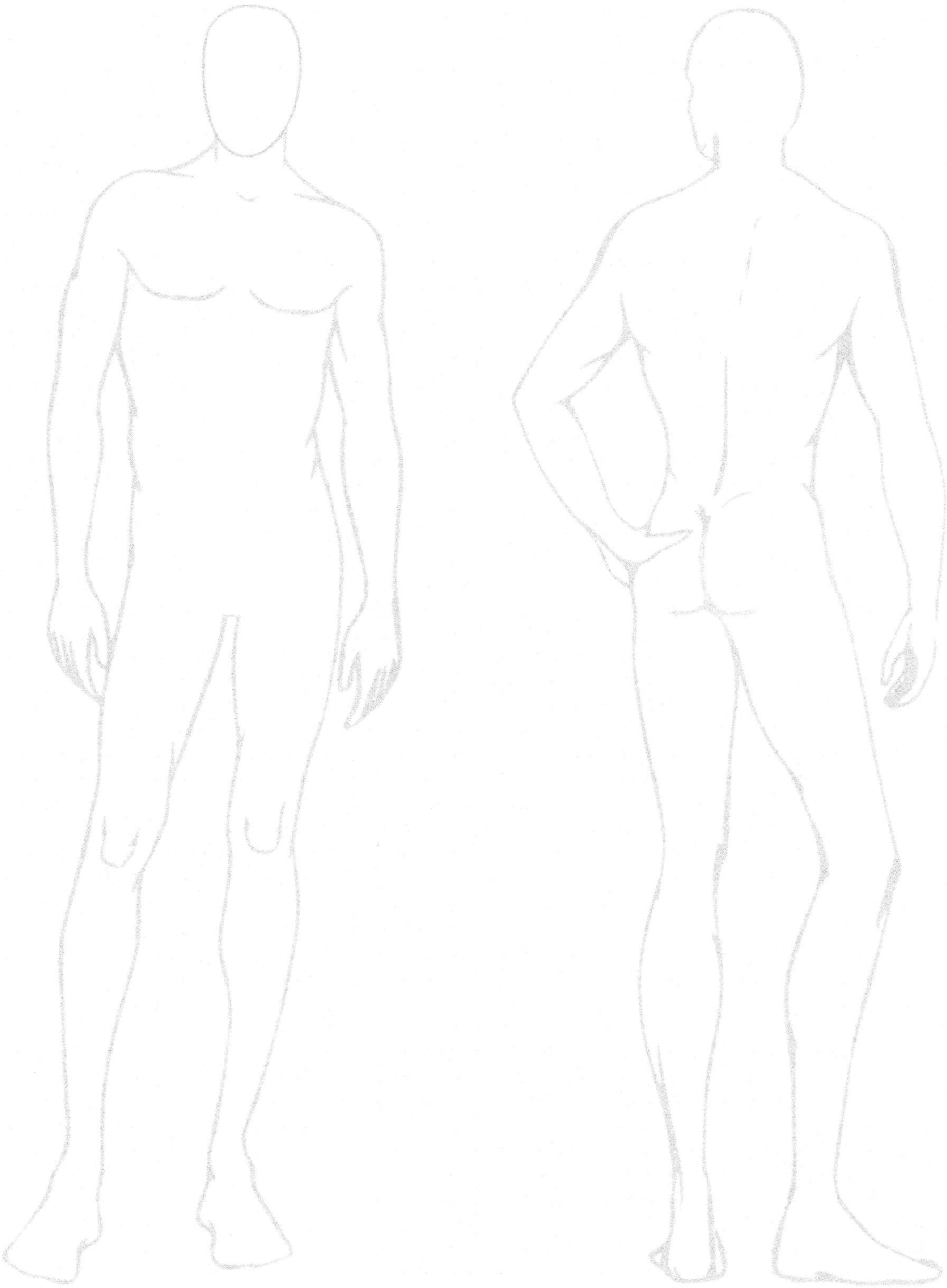

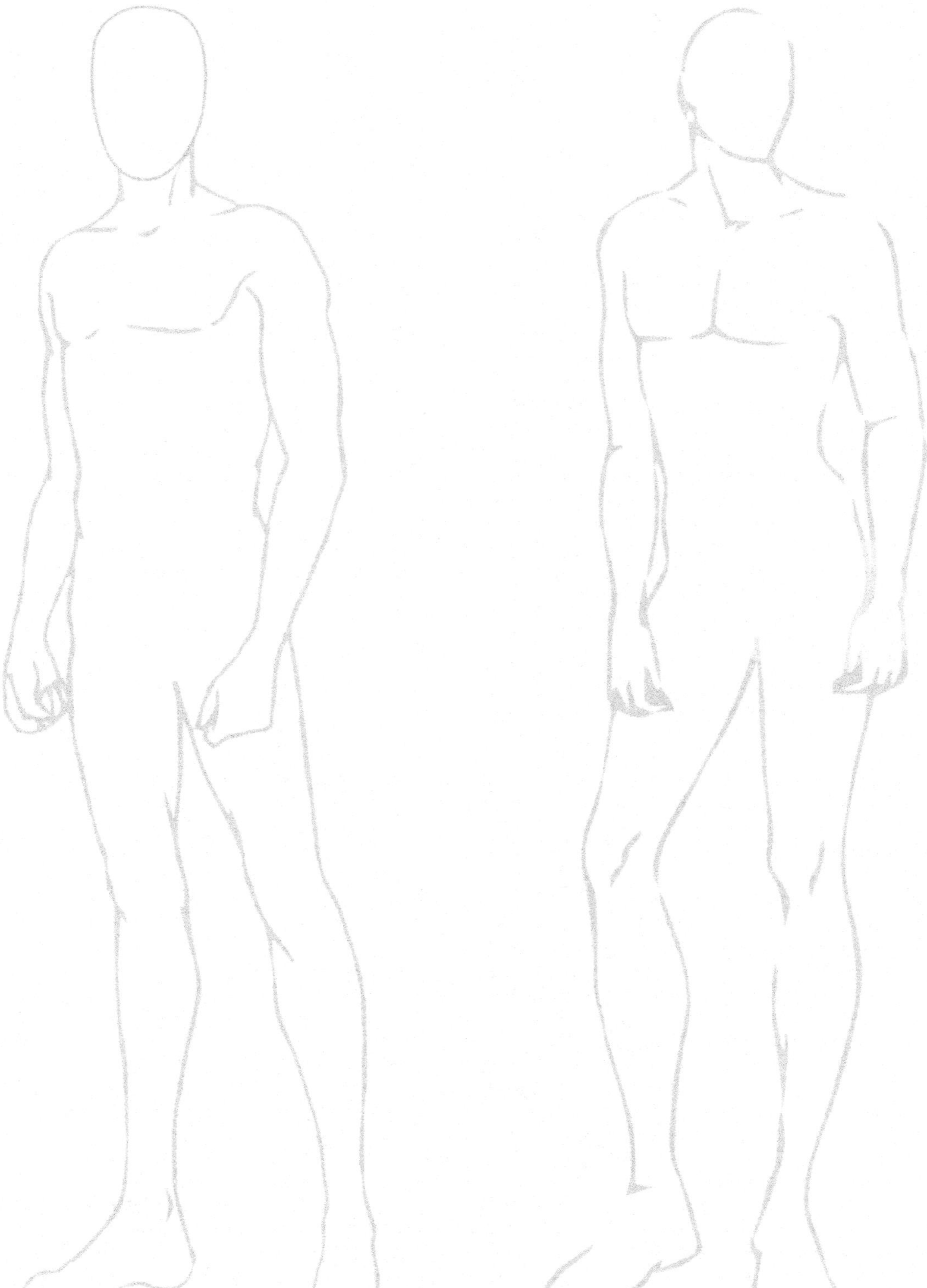

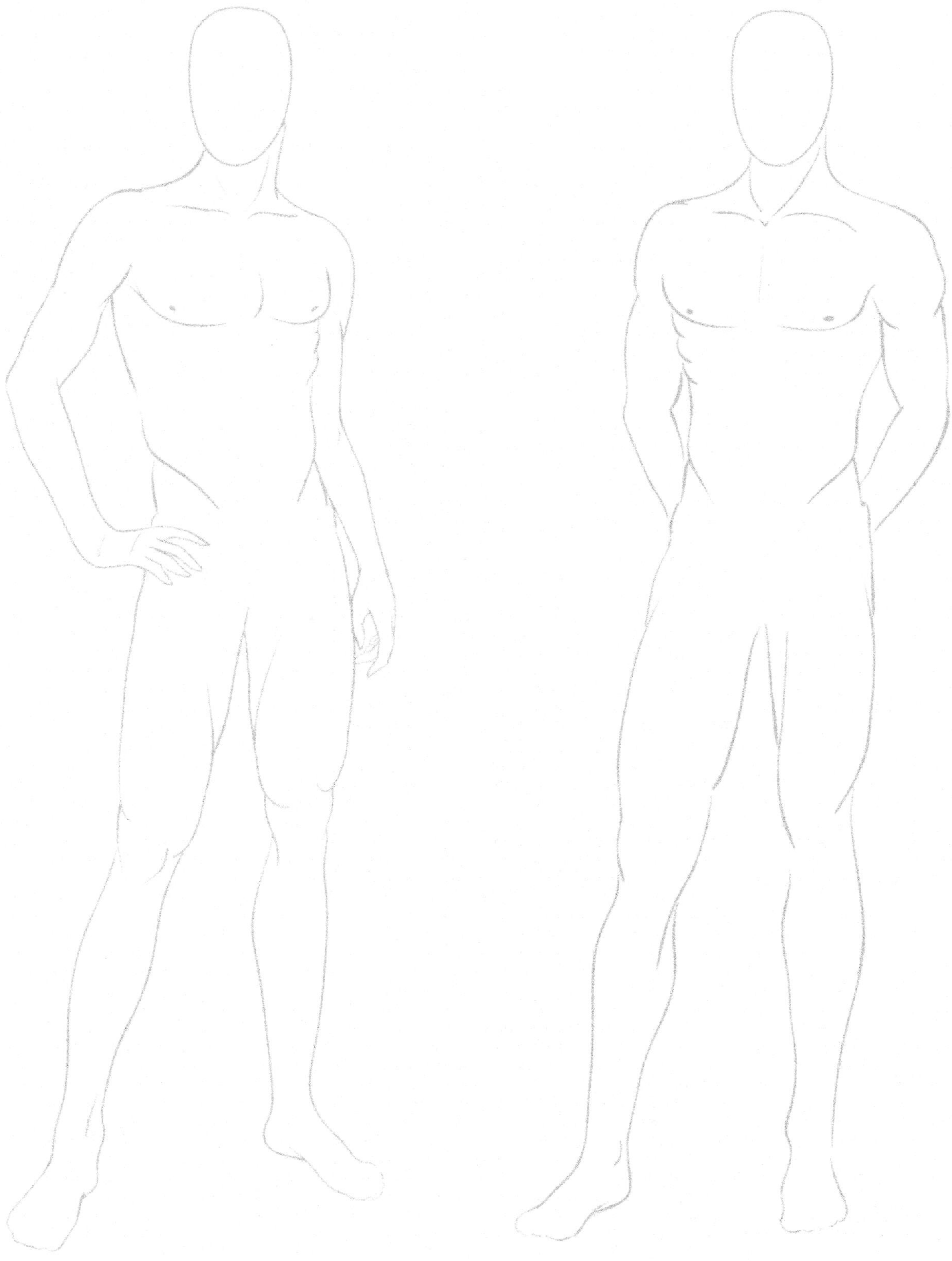

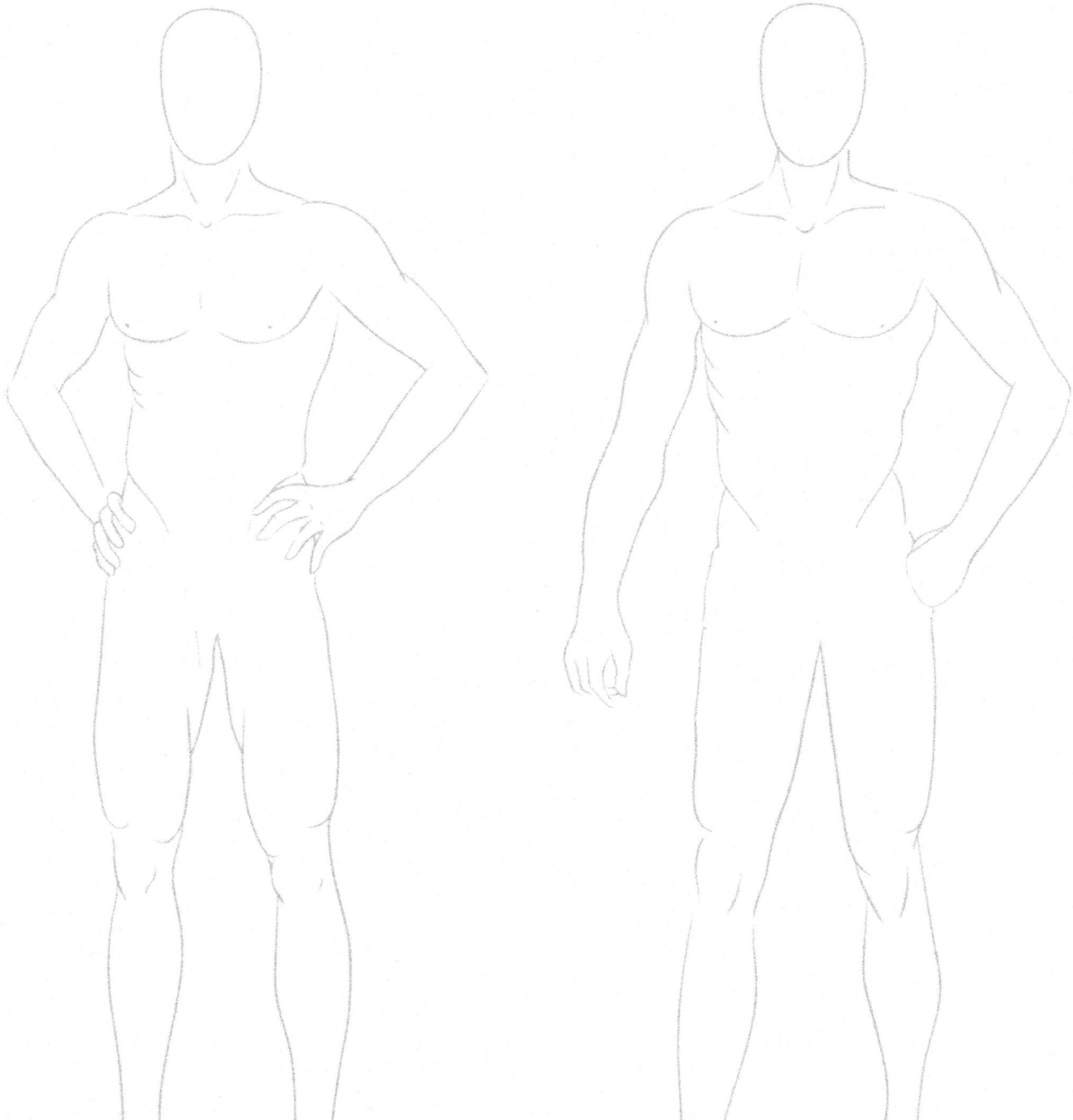

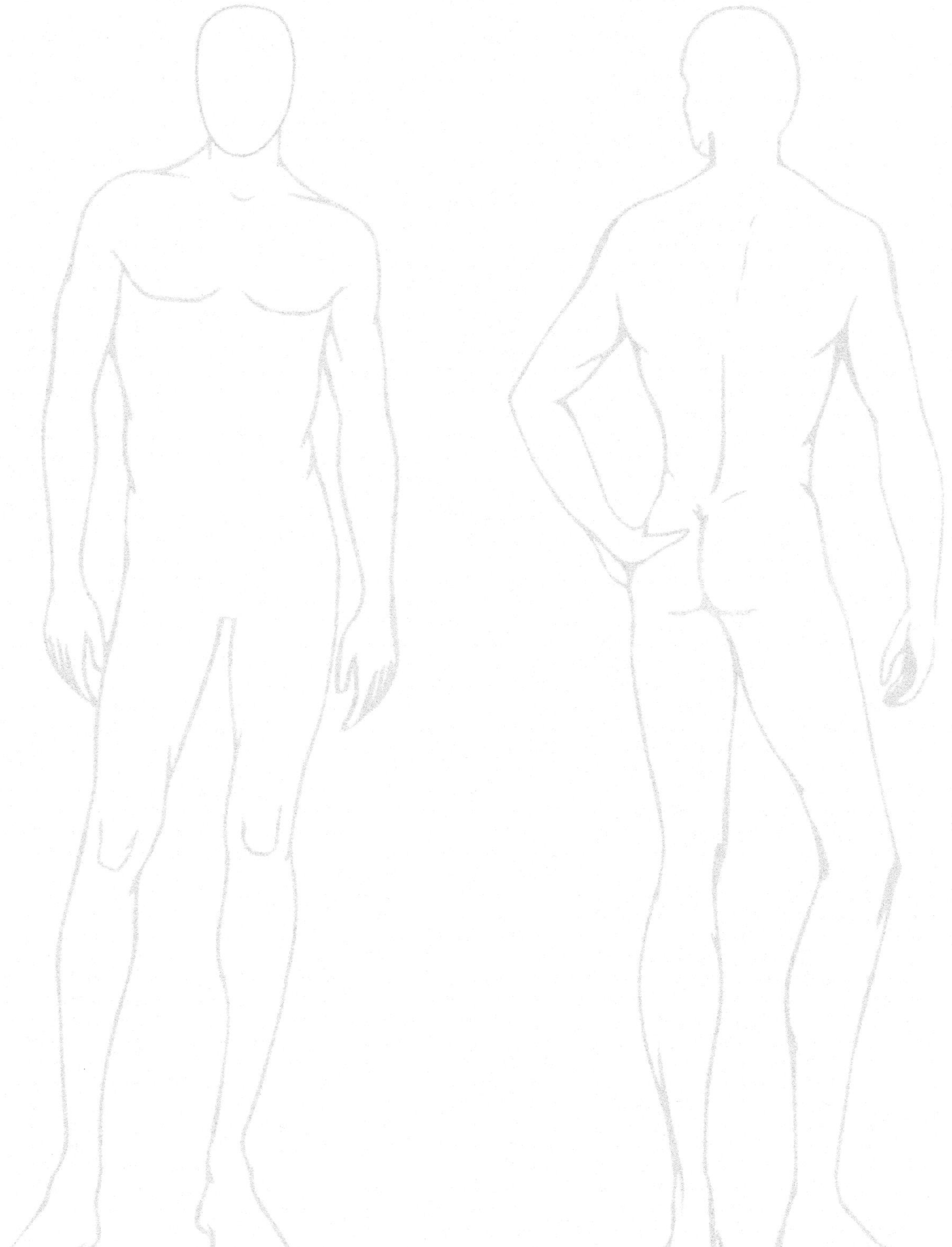

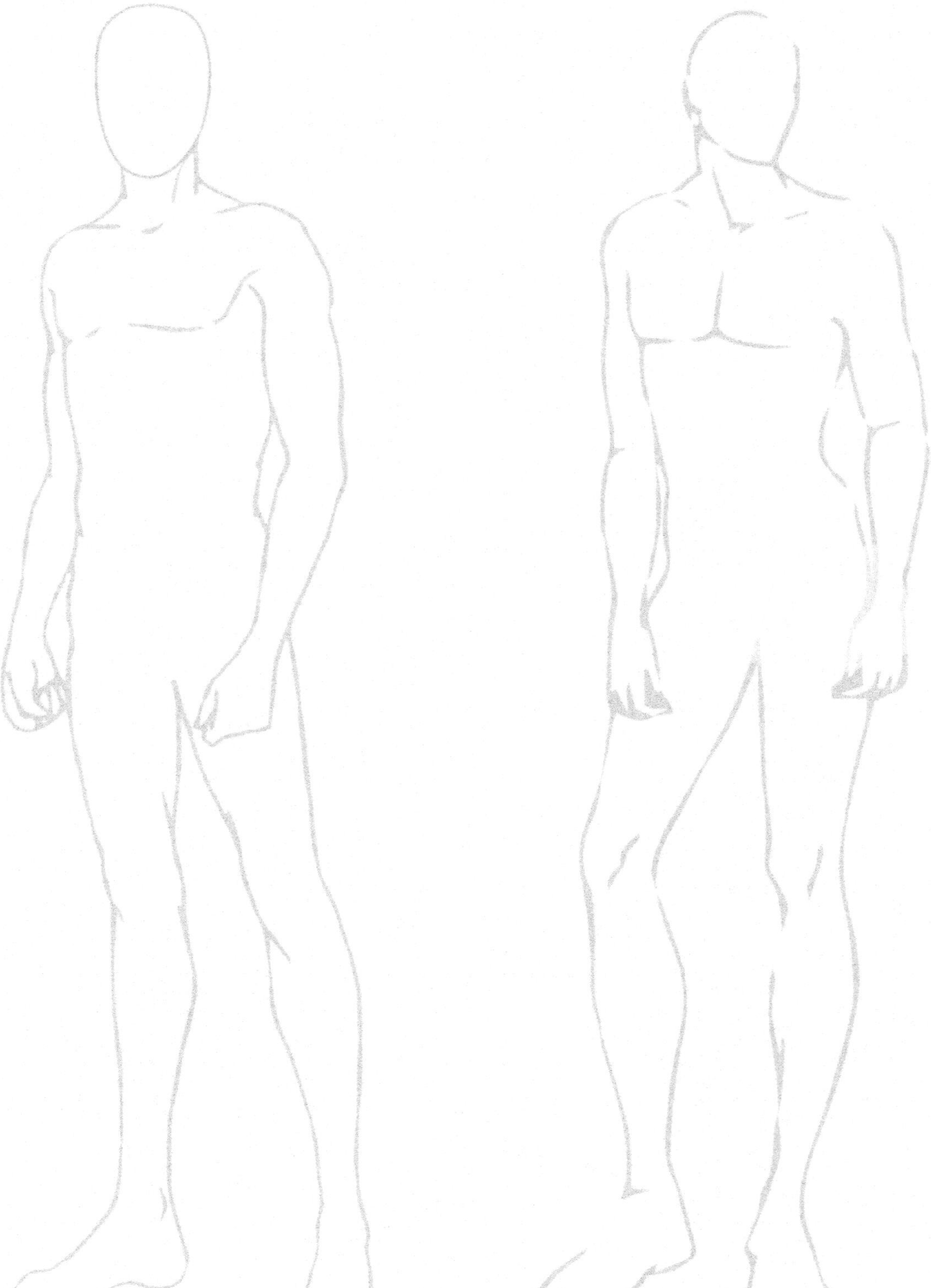

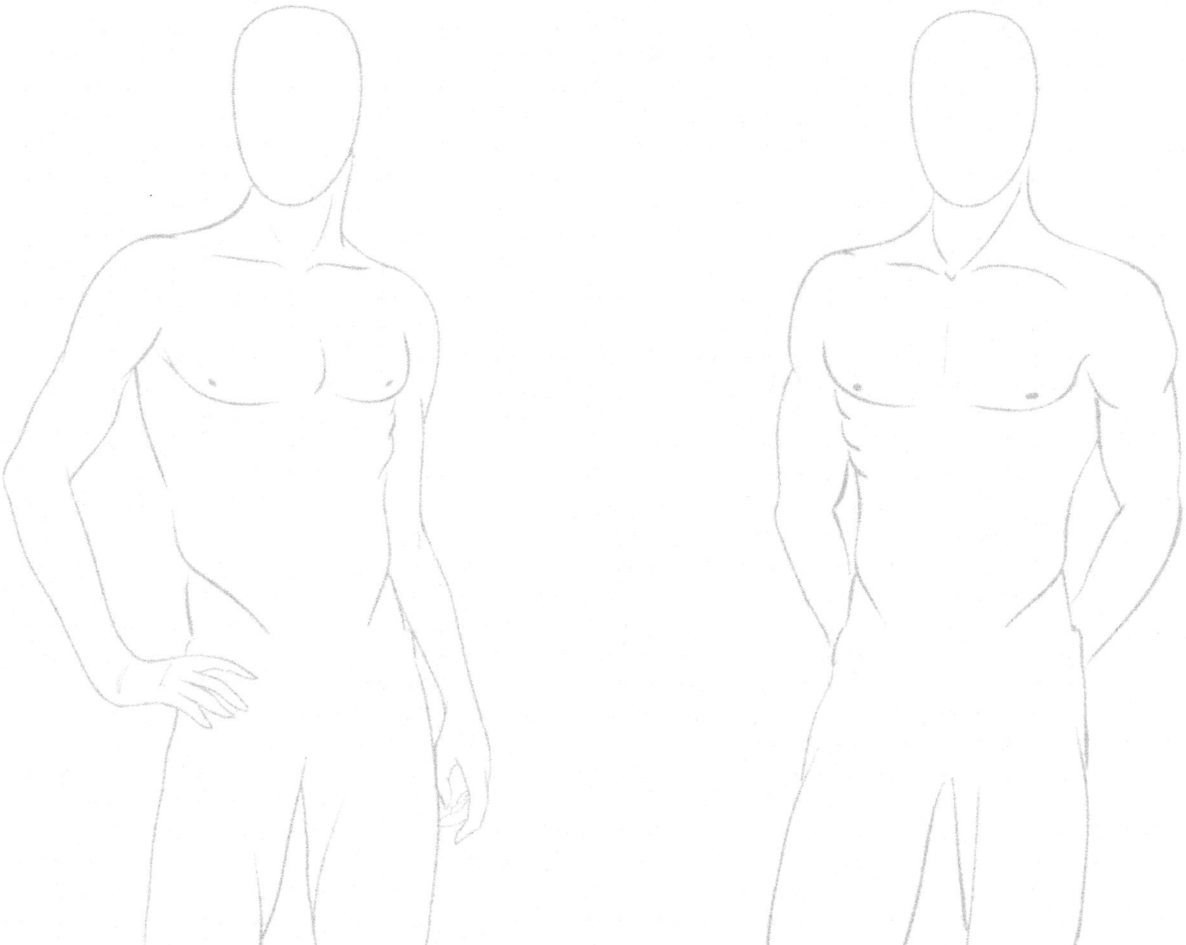

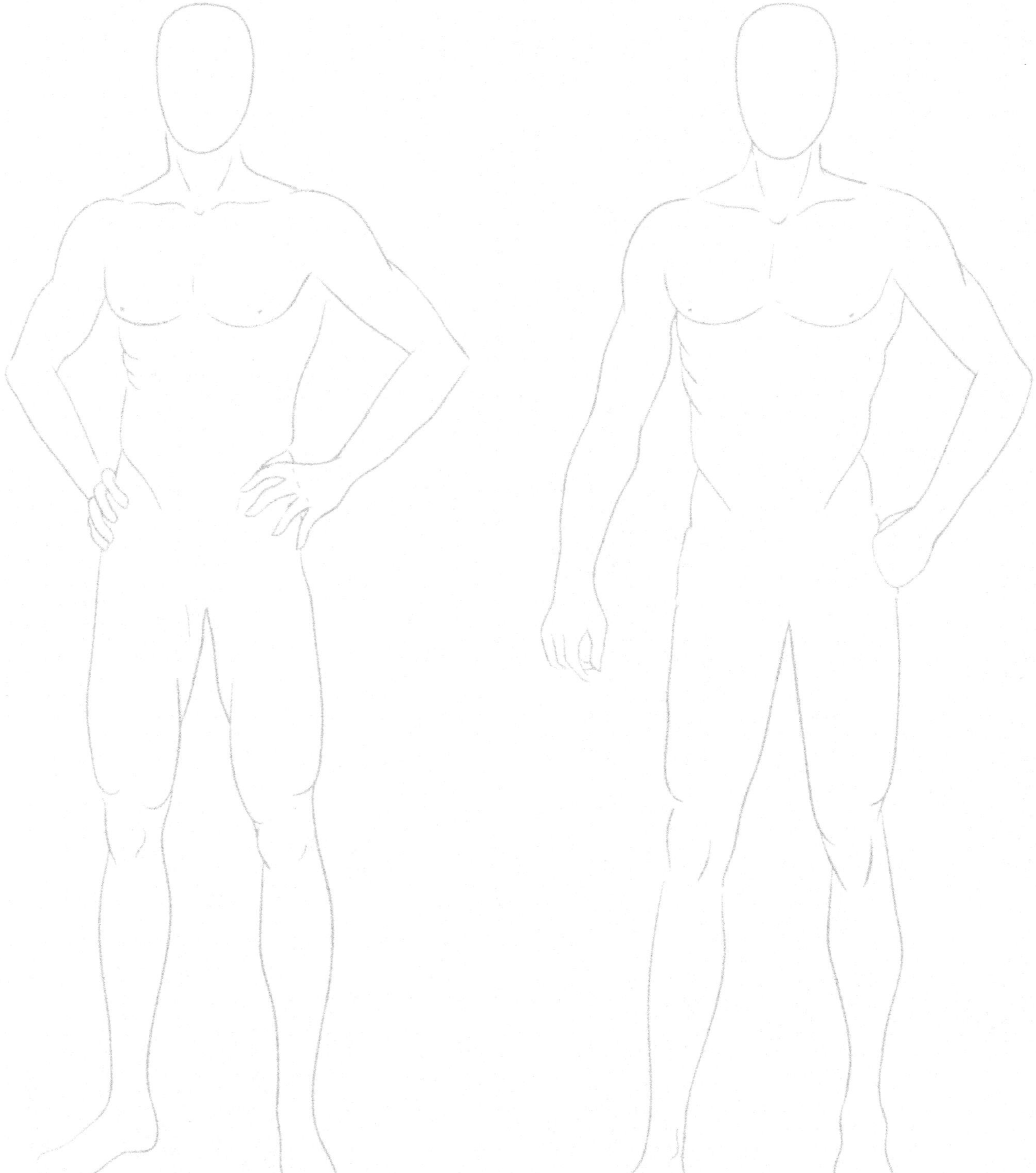

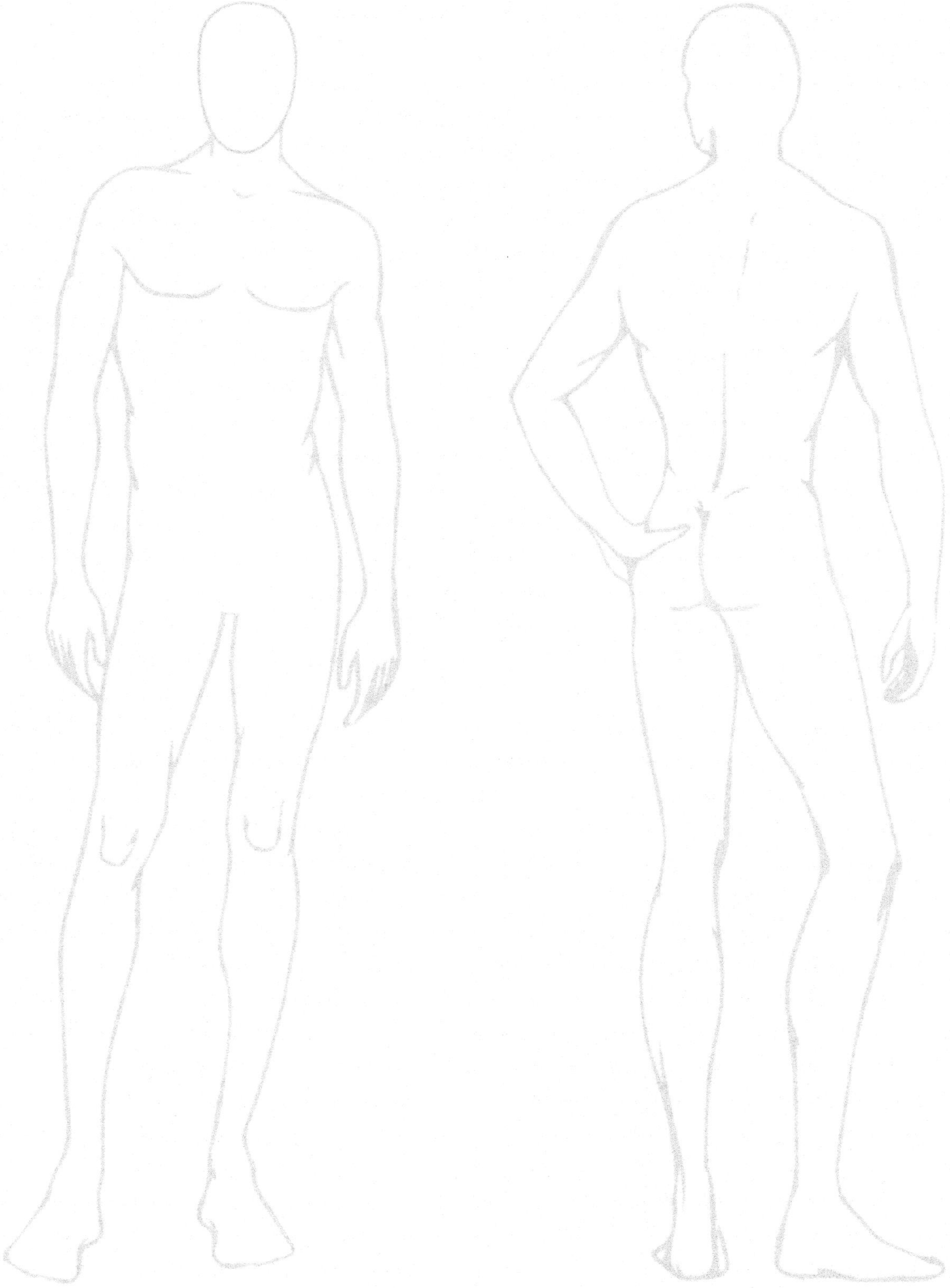

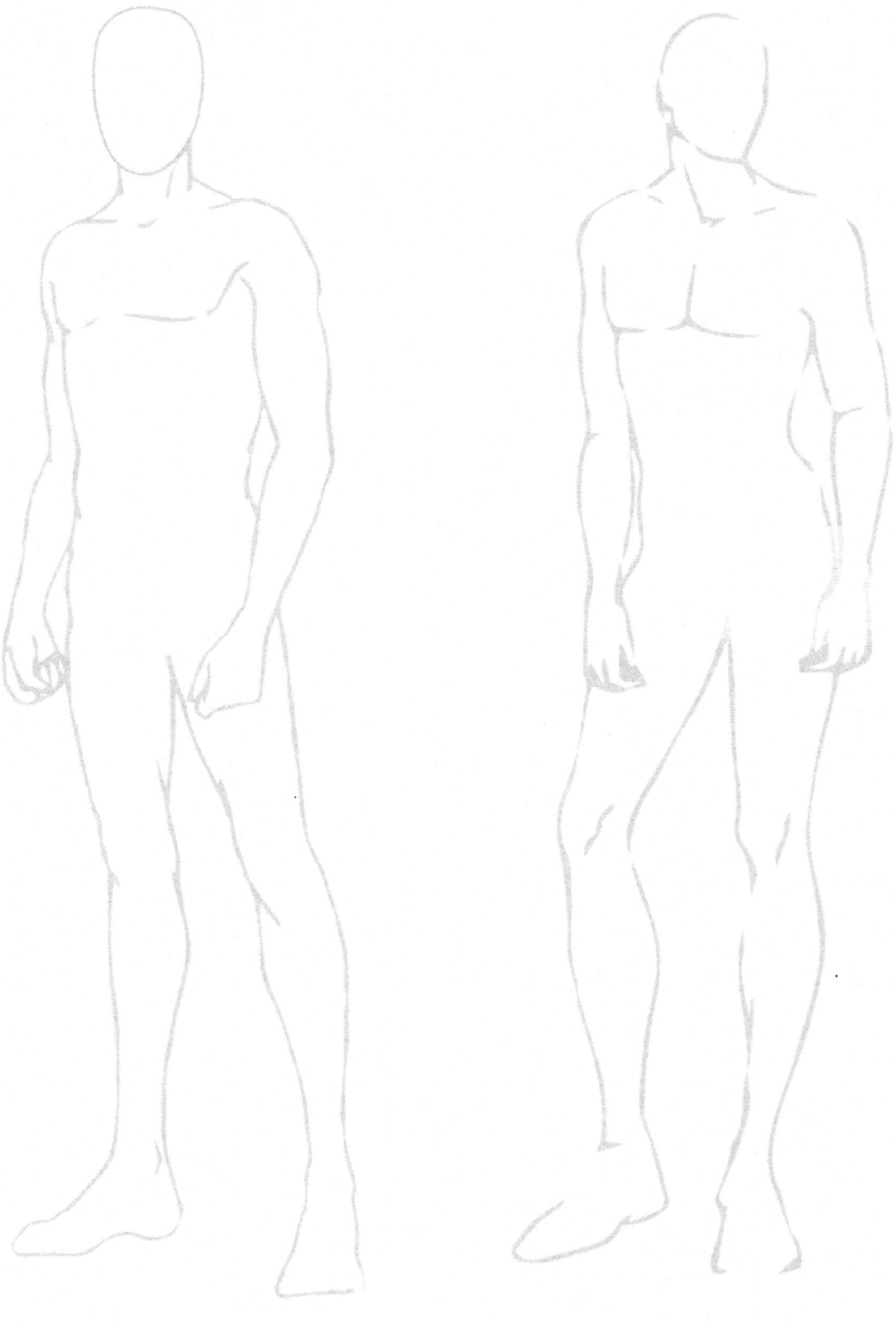